FINDING CUSTER

FINDING CUSTER

An American Icon's Journey from West Point
to the Little Bighorn

Stephen T. Powers
Kevin Dennehy

GTCI Press
Denver, Colorado

Finding Custer
First Printing
Copyright @ 2015, Stephen T. Powers and Kevin Dennehy
All rights reserved. No part of this publication may be reproduced, photocopied, stored in an unauthorized retrieval system, or transmitted in any form or by any means – including but not limited to; electronic, photocopy, audio/video recording without the prior written permission of the copyright holder.

Published by GTCI Press
Cover by Bright Sun Creative

ISBN-13: 978-0-9971105-0-0

*Steve Powers dedicates his efforts to the 1976 gang of four,
Julie, Greg, Robert and Bena,
who first helped him explore the
Little Bighorn Battlefield.*

*Kevin Dennehy dedicates his efforts to the U.S. Army's 7th
Cavalry Regiment.*

ACKNOWLEDGEMENTS

We would like to extend our heartfelt thanks to the following individuals who have aided us with the research and production of "Finding Custer."

Jim Brown
proprietor of
jim@brightsuncreative.com,
who produced our covers and maps

Jude De Lorca
proprietor of
One Hour Advisor - Words + Ideas
Consultant to Entrepreneurs and Small Business
jdelorca@onehouradvisor.com,
who helped us with editing

Patricia Shapiro
who helped with designing the publication

Christopher Kortlander and Putt Thompson,
who helped us understand the Little Bighorn battlefield

Kathryn Harrison, NPS,
who helped us explore the Washita battlefield

Dave Taylor
D1taylor@gmail.com
who professionally took photographs

TABLE OF CONTENTS

INTRODUCTION 11
A WARRIOR'S BEGINNINGS: THE OHIO AND MICHIGAN
YEARS 15
    NEW RUMLEY, OHIO 15
        Finding Custer in New Rumley...16
    MONROE, MICH. 18
        Finding Custer in Monroe, Mich...18
    UNITED STATES MILITARY ACADEMY AT WEST POINT 21
        Finding Custer at West Point 23

CUSTER IN THE CIVIL WAR: THE MAKING OF AN
AMERICAN LEGEND 27
        Brevet Rank — Political or Earned — or Both..............................29
    CUSTER AT GETTYSBURG 31
        A Quick Look at the Battle of Gettysburg 34
        Finding Custer Near Gettysburg..39
        Exploring the Gettysburg Battlefield 40
    CUSTER AFTER GETTYSBURG..42

INDIAN FIGHTER 48
    THE KANSAS INTERLUDE, 1868-72..48
    THE BATTLE OF THE WASHITA, NOVEMBER 27, 1868............54
        Finding Custer in Texas and Nebraska 63
        Custer's Engagements – Washita and Little Bighorn Rivers 65

ON TO MONTANA 69
    THE YELLOWSTONE EXPEDITION, 1873 69
        Finding Custer Along the Missouri and Yellowstone Rivers........73
    THE BLACK HILLS EXCURSION 1874......................................75
        Finding Custer in the Black Hills..79
        Other Interesting Destinations in the Black Hills 80
    POLITICS: 1875-76 82
    CENTENNIAL CAMPAIGN, 1876 84

    TO THE LITTLE BIGHORN, JUNE 22-25, 1876 91
        Following Custer to The Little Bighorn 92
    CUSTER HILL, JUNE 25, 1876 96
        Comanche 106

AFTERMATH 108
    Finding Custer at the Little Bighorn Battlefield National
    Monument, Crow Agency, Mont. 108
    Finding Custer Near the Little Bighorn Battlefield 114
    Custer's Officers Were a Varied Lot..119

LEGACY 121

APPENDICES 124
    1. PLAINS FORTS ASSOCIATED WITH THE CUSTERS 124
    2. A NOTE TO MILITARY FIREARMS IN THE CUSTER ERA ..141
    3. A FISTFUL OF FILMS ABOUT CUSTER..................................148

BIBLIOGRAPHY 153

ABOUT THE AUTHORS...157

NOTES 158

INTRODUCTION

How the world has changed in 39 years. When Steve Powers took his two teenaged children and a couple of their friends to Yellowstone National Park, by way of the Custer Battlefield National Monument in June of 1976, conflict was in the air. Only three years before, deadly violence had erupted at Wounded Knee. Now some of the same characters, Russell Means and his American Indian Movement (AIM) friends were threatening to disrupt the ceremonies planned for the centennial celebration of Custer's Last Stand.

As a military historian living in Colorado, Powers had long wanted to visit the Wyoming and Montana battlefields associated with the Plains Indian Wars. That summer the small group made a quick visit about a week before the anniversary date, then moved west to hike and fish in the Park. Fortunately, Means was content with speeches and posturing; one can imagine the Park Service heaved a sigh of relief.

But, Means and AIM were back in 1988, this time with a homemade plaque extolling the Indian victory in 1876 over the "U.S.Calvary" [sic]. (One must assume that this was a simple spelling error and not meant to imply that Custer Hill bears any relation to Golgotha.) But change, probably long overdue, was coming to the Custer Battlefield National Monument.

Contrast that time warp with the scene today. The battlefield has been renamed the Little Bighorn Battlefield National Monument, a Native American woman serves as its superintendent, an Indian casino occupies a prominent site just outside the Monument entrance, an Indian memorial stands just below Last Stand Hill and red granite steles (tablets) mark the spots where Indian warriors supposedly fell. The Little Big Horn Associates, a non-governmental association founded in 1966, initially opposed many of these changes. However, the LBHA recently sponsored a professionally conducted archeological survey of part of the battlefield, which survey information may well undermine what little is left of the Custer and 7th Cavalry mystique.

Yet, the Little Bighorn Battlefield continues to fascinate Americans and military historians. The parking lots at the monument are usually filled, as are the seats in the veranda behind the Visitor Center, where Park Rangers hold forth on a number of battlefield related topics. Histories of the campaign of 1876 continue to be published. Although the passions of the 1970s have cooled somewhat, the Little Bighorn Battlefield Monument still remains sacred ground to many Americans. We know it was manifested as such to Doug Keller, a former student of Powers who worked at the battlefield for years. Doug died April 2005 of brittle bone disease, an illness that had dwarfed his body, but not his mind or spirit. That one day almost 40 years ago, Powers had the unique experience of witnessing Doug give his lecture on the battle on the back veranda of the headquarters building.

Now, Powers and another talented, former-student and journalist, author and retired U.S. Army Colonel, Kevin Dennehy, have completed a new and comprehensive guidebook, "Finding Custer," which explores the career and locales associated with one of America's most celebrated and controversial military officers, George Armstrong Custer. We have included both the more famous sites as well as many of the more obscure.

In our chapter "Custer in the Civil War," we have concentrated on Custer at the Battle of Gettysburg. We realize that he heroically commanded Union cavalry forces in many other battles, but no monument or memorial exists to him at those sites today; for that reason, we have not included them. However, we do recommend that you visit those Civil War battlefields that were vital in establishing Custer's military reputation.

At the Battle of Gettysburg, Custer won accolades on the third, climatic day by turning back Robert E. Lee's "eyes and ears" — J.E.B. Stuart's "Gray Ghosts." Besides you will find that Gettysburg is a great day trip from Washington, Baltimore or other nearby eastern cities.

Our guidebook prominently features Armstrong during his western campaigns. We do reach our own conclusions about his conduct in our "Legacy" chapter, not only for his earlier campaigns, but for the disaster at the Little Bighorn as well.

We realize there have been hundreds of books published about Custer —what he did or failed to do — but our guidebook, in addition to tracing his military career and taking you to the major sites associated with that career, will help you find nearby hotels, restaurants and other places of interest.

As with any guidebook, changes will occur after publication. Please let us know if you find something we need to update by going to our website, www.militaryhistorytraveller.com. We hope you enjoy our new guidebook.

Stephen T. Powers
Kevin Dennehy

Denver, Colorado
December 2015

A WARRIOR'S BEGINNINGS: THE OHIO AND MICHIGAN YEARS

NEW RUMLEY, OHIO

The Custers sprang from a Rhineland immigrant family, Küster, who arrived in North America at the end of the 17th century. A branch of the family eventually established roots in New Rumley, Ohio, where, on Dec. 5, 1839, Maria Ward Kirkpatrick (1807-1882), wife of Emmanuel Henry Custer (1806-1892), gave birth to a son, George Armstrong Custer, one of her seven children. Little is known today about Custer's early years in New Rumley, but one legend has it that he gave himself the nickname "Autie" when he couldn't pronounce "Armstrong." Most accounts of young Autie state that he was a poor student who was always playing pranks and involved in other mischief. However, there is one important exception — younger brother Nevin told interviewers that Autie was a quiet boy, preferring to read history rather than participating in the shenanigans of his other brothers. But, Nevin's recollections don't ring true given Autie's almost juvenile penchant for playing jokes on his younger brothers throughout his life. In any event, Custer was born and grew up in an old log cabin, formerly a stagecoach tavern owned by his maternal grandfather, which had been expanded with a wood frame addition. The original structure was torn down in the late 19th century and another house built in the same spot, but, when Custer's birth site was designated a state memorial in 1932, the existing house, replacement or not, was moved down the road into town. The Custer clan had not occupied a high rung on New Rumley's socio-economic ladder.

Finding Custer in New Rumley

Today, a statue of Custer, sculpted by Erwin Frey, is located along State Route 646 and Chrisman Road on New Rumley's west side. The memorial, of which it forms a part, is maintained by the Ohio Historical Society and features the statue, an exhibit pavilion with information about Custer's life plus the foundations of his birth home. In 1932, Custer's widow, Elizabeth (Libbie) Bacon Custer, was in her nineties, living alone on Park Avenue in New York City, when the statue in New Rumley was dedicated. Because of her health, Libbie chose not to attend the ceremonies, but, according to contemporary accounts, she spoke to the gathered crowd in New Rumley via a loudspeaker connected to a telephone line. Ever protective of her husband's image, she privately professed not to like the new statue that depicted Autie wearing a short cape, saying it made him look foppish.

In the 1940s, the Ohio Historical Society erected a second memorial to Custer in the center of the town. The Custer Memorial Association oversees both the memorial and a museum that is housed in the former Methodist Church. Museum admission is free and it is open Monday through Sunday during daylight hours. The site is also open for events, by appointment, on the last Sunday of summer months from 1 p.m. to 4 p.m.
Website: https://www.ohiohistory.org/visit/museum-and-site-locator/custer-monument.

Annual festivals in New Rumley include Custer Day, which is usually the first Saturday in June; and the Custer Birthday Celebration, the first Saturday in December.

For $10 annual dues you can become a member of the

Association, which meets on the third Monday of the month excepting June and December. Contact the Association at P. O. Box 111, New Rumley, Ohio 43984.

Travel Resources for New Rumley
While being described by some as "being in the middle of nowhere," today New Rumley is a quick trip from Cleveland or Pittsburg. The town is located a short distance west of Steubenville, Ohio. Affordable lodging and meals can be found throughout Harrison County. Information can be obtained at: http://www.visitharrisoncounty.com/our-county/new-rumley/.

Custer Memorial, New Rumley, Ohio. Libbie said it made him look "foppish." The statue's pedestal reads: "General George Armstrong Custer, born in New Rumley Harrison County Ohio December 5 1839 -- Killed in battle with the indians [sic] on the Little Bighorn -- Montana June 25 1876." (Photo: Wikimedia)

We do know that young Autie formed a strong attachment to his older half-sister, Lydia Ann Kirkpatrick, and after her marriage to David Reed visited her often in her new home in Monroe, Mich. During his early years, he bounced around between New Rumley and Monroe before, at age 14, moving into Ann's household and remaining there for two years. At age 16, Custer was back in Ohio attending the McNeely Normal School, later renamed the Hopedale Normal College. While attending McNeely, Custer was said to have worked in the local coal mines to pay for room and board. After graduating from McNeely in 1856, Custer briefly taught school in nearby Cadiz, Ohio. While there are no formal memorials to Custer in Hopedale or Cadiz, streets, an old defunct hotel and even a pharmacy are named after him.

MONROE, MICH.

Custer not only largely grew up in Monroe, but it was there that he also courted and married Elizabeth "Libbie" Bacon (1842-1933), the daughter of a prominent Monroe jurist. Monroe also remains a significant place in Custer family lore, not just because Autie grew up there, but because many members of his immediate family, including Libbie for a time, continued to reside in the vicinity after his death at the Little Bighorn.

Finding Custer in Monroe, Mich.

In 1910, Libbie and President William Howard Taft dedicated an equestrian statue of Custer in Monroe that now stands at the corner of Elm and Monroe Streets. Various Monroe streets, historic markers, city limit signs, buildings and schools — and even the local airport — are named for the town's most illustrious son.

Custer statue, "Toward the Enemy," in Monroe, Mich. (Photo: Wikimedia)

Traveler Resources for Monroe
Monroe, founded in 1785 (Michigan's third-oldest city) and with a population of 23,000, is located off Interstate 75, 17 miles north of Toledo, Ohio, and 35 miles south of Detroit. General information on lodging, restaurants and attractions can be found at: http://www.monroeinfo.com/.

   Monroe hosts the annual Custer Week that celebrates and pays tribute to the life of Custer and his family. The event takes place during the first full week of October and features activities, music events and presentations for school children at the Monroe County Historical Museum. Other activities include concerts, reenactments, the annual Custer's First Run 5k Race, and more.

   In the past, Steve Alexander, the country's leading Custer reenactor, has led the General Custer Walking Tour, the event that kicks off Custer Week in Monroe. He also does reenactments as well at the Little Bighorn Battlefield and The Custer Battlefield Museum at Garyowen. The Alexanders (Steve's wife, Sandy, also does an impersonation of Libbie Custer) live in the Bacon home that originally stood at 126 South Monroe Street before it was moved in 1911 to its present location on Cass Street. See Alexander's web site at georgecuster.com; for information on the Custer and Bacon homes in Monroe, visit the web site, www.custerlives.com

Monroe County Historical Museum
This small museum's displays highlight the early history of Monroe, the life of George Armstrong Custer, Indian lore and other special topics. Summer hours: 10 a.m. to 5 p.m., daily; winter hours: 10 a.m. to 5 p.m., Wednesday through Sundays. Group tours for 30 or more last about an hour. Reservations necessary. Fee for admission Memorial Day through Labor Day. 126 S. Monroe St., Monroe, 48161; Phone: (734) 240-7780. http://www.co.monroe.mi.us/government/departments_offices/museum/index.html

Woodland Cemetery, Custer Family Plot
Woodland Cemetery is located at the south end of Monroe's Jerome Street. Signs lead to the Custer Family Plot. Buried here are Libbie's parents, Judge Daniel and Eleanor Bacon, Armstrong's parents, Emmanuel and Maria Custer, and his sister Margaret. The graves of younger brother, Boston, and nephew Harry "Autie" Reed are also found here. Both young men died at the Little Bighorn, where they were originally buried before being moved to Woodland in 1878.

Custer Family Plot in Monroe, Michigan (Photo: Wikimedia)

UNITED STATES MILITARY ACADEMY AT WEST POINT, N.Y.

Just after finishing his formal schooling in Ohio, the 17-year-old Autie fell madly in love with Miss Mary Jane Holland. Her father strongly disapproved of the relationship and, as one story goes, in order to be rid of young Custer, asked a friend, Republican Congressman John Bingham, to award him with an appointment to the United States Military Academy. In reality, Custer, already enamored with military history and coming from a relatively poor and obscure Ohio farm family, viewed an appointment to West Point as a means of social and economic advancement. So fate, and possibly Custer's amorous behavior, put him on the path to a military career — and destiny.

Custer entered West Point in 1858 as a member of the class of 1862. Three years later, he emerged last in his class of 34 cadets, graduated early because of the U.S. Army's desperate need for trained junior officers. His time at the Point, mercifully one might add, had been cut short by a year because of the outbreak of the Civil War.

Young Cadet Custer at West Point (Wikimedia)

Custer's lack of discipline as a Cadet has been well documented over the many decades since his death. He tested the boundaries of a strict institution, racking up a record 726 demerits and, as a result, spent an inordinate amount of time serving extra duty. He was on the verge being expelled during all three years because of his many disciplinary infractions and academic deficiencies, but, as his numerous biographers have pointed out, when his back was to the wall, he managed to avoid dismissal. In the 19th century, a bottom-of-the-class ranking at West Point usually meant a posting to an obscure infantry regiment, however Custer's skill in horsemanship soon opened up a different career path. No matter what else contemporaries may have thought of Custer as a soldier or as a person, no one ever denied that he was a skilled and tireless horseman.

The Military Academy was in disarray in the spring of 1861 as many southern cadets resigned in order to enlist in their states' newly organized military forces. Custer, as one would expect of a mid-westerner, remained loyal to the Union. Immediately after graduation, he caught the train to Washington, D.C., where he reported to the War Department for assignment.

Finding Custer at West Point

The United States Military Academy, founded in 1802 during Thomas Jefferson's first administration, was the site of a strategic Revolutionary War fort on the Hudson River. Then called Fort Clinton, it encompassed several smaller fortifications, including Fort Putnam (preserved today in its Revolutionary War configuration) that guarded a chain barrier stretched across the river. In a famous incident that forever branded him as the American arch-traitor, Gen. Benedict Arnold attempted to betray the Fort to the British in exchange for a commission in the British Army as a Brigadier General and £20,000. Of course, the plot failed, but Arnold did receive his Generalship and a sum over £6,000 (the British reneged on the full amount because the plot was unsuccessful!)

The Academy, colloquially known as West Point because of its site on the Hudson River, is located next to the town of

Highland Falls in Orange County, one hour's drive north of New York City. Within 20 minutes of the post are Revolutionary War sites, local wineries, Storm King Art Center, Boscobel House & Gardens, West Point Tours, Woodbury Common Premium Shopping Outlets and other attractions. General information on lodging, restaurants and attractions can be found at: http://www.orangetourism.org/.

West Point Museum
The West Point Museum is not just focused on the history of the United States Military Academy and the U.S. Army, but also contains exhibits concerning warfare through the ages. The Museum opened its doors in the 1850s, hallmarking it as the oldest military museum in the United States.

The Museum is located outside the gates of the Academy, adjacent to the Visitor's Center, where one can sign up for a tour of the Academy that includes its history and a visit to the parade ground, Trophy Point and the Chapel. One of the Museum's prized possessions is the last message from Custer to Captain Frederick Benteen. Displayed in a museum case, the message, delivered by Pvt. John Martin and hastily scrawled by Custer's aide, Lt. W.W. Cooke, reads: "Benteen. Come on. Big village. Be Quick. Bring pack. W.W. Cooke. PS bring pacs."

Free admission. Open Monday-Sunday, 10:30 a.m. to 4:15 p.m. Closed Thanksgiving, Christmas and New Year's Day. Phone: (845) 938-3590, e-mail: museum@usma.edu, website: www.usma.edu.

West Point Cemetery
The Cemetery was a burial ground for Revolutionary War soldiers long before it was officially dedicated in 1817. Notable burials include Winfield Scott, James Gavin, William Westmoreland, Norman Schwarzkopf and, of course, George Armstrong Custer.

Custer's grave at West Point (Photo: Wikimedia). His wife, Elizabeth Bacon, is buried beside him. An unrealistic statue, depicting Custer with both sword and revolver in hand by J. Wilson MacDonald, detested by Libbie, originally marked his grave. After persistent lobbying by Libbie, it was removed in 1884 by Gen. Wesley Merritt, the retiring superintendent of the Military Academy.

Custer was first interred on the Little Bighorn battlefield two days after his death. His remains were moved east in the summer of 1877 and, on October 10th, were shipped by steamer down the Hudson from Poughkeepsie to the Academy. Thousands of mourners lined the route. His coffin was exhibited in the Post Chapel prior to reburial, which Libbie attended, escorted by West Point Superintendent Maj. Gen. John Schofield, as did his father and other family members. Armstrong's grave is marked by an ornate stone obelisk with Libbie's flat grave marker resting next to it.

The Thayer Hotel
Located just outside the main gate, the Thayer Hotel has been an iconic part of the Academy since 1926 and provides comfortable accommodations for the visitor. The Thayer is listed on the National Registry of Historic Places and commands great views of the Hudson River. The Hotel boasts complimentary Wi-Fi, valet parking, and beverage service in the main lobby. Other amenities include MacArthur's Riverview Restaurant, Patton's Tavern and Zulu Lounge rooftop bar. Address: 674 Thayer Road, West Point, N.Y. 10996, Phone: (800) 247-5047, e-mail: info@thethayerhotel.com , web: www.thethayerhotel.com.

The town of Highland Falls also provides numerous other accommodations and restaurants for the traveler. See various travel accommodation websites such as TripAdvisor.com, Booking.com or Hotels.com for ratings, availability and prices.

CUSTER IN THE CIVIL WAR: THE MAKING OF AN AMERICAN LEGEND

The Civil War gave George Armstrong Custer the opportunity to forge his name in blood and steel in the psyche of the American people. He skillfully led cavalrymen in many of major battles of the Army of the Potomac from First Bull Run to Appomattox Court House. He served under general officers who would have direct influence on his later success and failures, including Gens. Philip Sheridan, Alfred Pleasonton and George McClellan, all of whom would further his meteoric career.

Custer with West Point classmate and Confederate prisoner, Lt. James Washington at Fair Oaks, Va. (Photo: Wikimedia, Library of Congress)

Coming off an undistinguished stint as a West Point cadet, as soon as the newly minted 2nd Lt. Custer arrived in Washington he was assigned the 2nd U.S. Cavalry and immediately detailed by Army commander Gen. Winfield Scott to carry dispatches to Maj. Gen. Irvin McDowell. Completing that task, he joined his regiment and was immediately thrown into the fighting at the disastrous First Battle of Bull Run.

Custer survived the debacle and during the remainder of 1861 he showed personal gallantry as he was frequently transferred among different units as the need arose. Soon after First Bull Run, he was promoted to 1st Lt. and reassigned the 5th U.S. Cavalry (the old 2nd redesignated), where he served for a time on the staff of Brig. Gen. Philip Kearny. (West Point graduates were often given staff assignments because they had some acquaintance with military protocol.) In early October 1861, Armstrong was granted a leave of absence for an illness, the nature of which remains obscure today. A letter survives in which he wrote that he thought, at a low point, he was going to die. He spent his convalescence in Monroe where he courted Libbie Bacon and Fanny Fifield, among other eligible young women. After an embarrassing drunken episode, he also made a life-changing decision when he promised his sister Ann, that he would become a teetotaler, a promise that he kept for the rest of his life. Whatever the malady, Armstrong rejoined the army in February 1862, apparently fully recovered, in time to serve with distinction, if in relative obscurity, during McClellan's ill-fated Peninsula Campaign. But, fame came quickly after he volunteered to lead a small reconnaissance force of mixed cavalry and infantry (4th Michigan), across the Chickahominy River near New Bridge, Va. to probe the Confederate position. His reconnaissance was deemed a success when his infantrymen captured some 50 Confederates, whereupon McClellan personally commended Custer for his gallantry (first across the river and the last to leave). McClellan moved him from Brig.

Gen. William F. Smith's staff to his own as an aide-de-camp with the rank of brevet captain, effective May 28, 1862. Young Armstrong came to idolize "Little Mac," but his personal circumstance changed rapidly when President Lincoln sacked McClellan as Commander of the Army of the Potomac in November and appointed Gen. Ambrose E. Burnside in his place. With his staff position gone, along with his brevet rank, Lt. Custer returned to his home in Ohio to await reassignment, meanwhile ardently pursuing Libbie Bacon.

Brevet Rank — Political or Earned — or Both?

Brevet rank, authorized by the 1775 Articles of War and first used by the Continental Army during the Revolutionary War, was a means of temporarily promoting officers above their normal rank for merit or new command responsibilities. Early brevet commissions often were given to foreign officers, while other brevet promotions were awarded for "meritorious conduct" during the course of the war. Brevet rank, or brevets, had no effect within an officer's unit, but when assigned a duty at the new rank, the officer could command higher pay. After the War of 1812, just as with other Presidential commissions, brevet rank also required confirmation by the U.S. Senate. For most of the 19th century brevet promotions were common in the regular army because Congress sharply limited the number of officers who could serve in each rank. Brevet promotions allowed the Army to temporarily exceed that number.

During the Civil War, the rules and regulations for brevet promotions were vague at best. The use of brevet rank was certainly excessive as many senior officers received some sort of brevet designation, some even posthumously. Brevets were conferred for either gallantry or meritorious service, both of which could be very subjective.

After an 1863 congressional act, both Regular Army (RA)

and Volunteer Army officers could receive brevet rank. Often, individuals held RA rank and brevets in both branches. For example, an officer might hold the brevet rank of Brigadier General of Volunteers, while remaining at the RA rank of Captain as did Custer in 1863. Obviously, the bestowing of brevets on Armstrong Custer, Wesley Merritt and Elon Farnsworth promoted them over officers with higher rank, thus allowing them to command units (in this case, volunteer cavalry brigades) normally assigned to general officers. When Custer was breveted to Major General of Volunteers in September 1864, enabling him to command the volunteer Third Cavalry Division, he soon after was promoted to brevet Colonel in the RA to reward him for his outstanding combat leadership at Third Winchester. His official rank in the RA remained that of Captain.

After the Civil War, brevet ranks became honorary titles, which included no command authority or increased pay. Active duty officers reverted back to their lower RA ranks at the end of the war. Congress was forced to legislate those usages because of the confusion and dissention they were creating.

Custer was an exception — when he requested reactivation in 1866 with the rank of colonel (his brevet RA rank at the war's conclusion) to command one of the new cavalry regiments, he was instead commissioned with the RA rank of lieutenant colonel, which made him second in command of the 7th Cavalry, but a far cry from the brevet rank of Major General of Volunteers he had held the year before.

By the close of the 19th century, the practice of breveting disappeared from the U.S. Army, and also the U.S. Marine Corps, which also had used brevets during the Civil War. Today, all branches of the U.S. military, except the Air Force, are allowed to "frock" officers into the rank of the position they hold before the official promotion date.

Burnside, whose tenure as army commander didn't survive the Union disaster at the Battle of Fredericksburg in December 1862, was replaced by Gen. Joseph Hooker who, in turn, was out-Generaled by Gens. Lee and Jackson at Chancellorsville in May 1863.

If his lot in life had improved under Little Mac's command, it was enhanced even further when he reported to his new commander, Maj. Gen. Alfred E. Pleasonton who commanded a cavalry division. Pleasonton placed the young lieutenant on his staff and served as a mentor who allowed Armstrong to observe the political machinations that went with senior command.

Capt. Custer (he resumed his brevet rank when Pleasonton received his second star) accompanied Pleasonton, who was named commander of the Cavalry Corps after the Battle of Chancellorsville, through the Shenandoah Valley at the beginning of the Gettysburg Campaign. Custer fought at Aldie and Brandy Station during the run up to that epic battle.

CUSTER AT GETTYSBURG

At this critical moment in the war and the future of the United States, Lincoln took a bold and dangerous move of replacing Hooker with Gen. George G. Meade, serving as commander of the Army's Fifth Corps. This shake-up reverberated through the Army, as Maj. Gen. Julius Stahel, commander of the cavalry force guarding Washington, was dismissed along with Brig. Gen. Joseph Copeland, commander of the Michigan Brigade (cavalry). Pleasonton, who had lobbied for the reassignments, then assumed command of the entire cavalry force. As new cavalry commander Pleasonton needed capable field officers to command units of his reorganized corps, so he turned to three promising young captains on his staff, Wesley Merritt, Elon Farnsworth and Armstrong Custer, proposing to Meade that they all be given the brevet rank of Brigadier General of Volunteers.

(Note: Custer and Merritt amply lived up to Pleasonton's high expectations; Farnsworth was killed during the Battle of Gettysburg leading a foolhardy charge ordered by his superior, Brig. Gen. Judson Kilpatrick.) Meade concurred and with a telegraphed message to Gen. Henry Halleck in Washington made brevet Capt. George Armstrong Custer a Brigadier General of Volunteers, at 23 the youngest general officer in the Army.

A surprised Custer, who had earlier been turned down for promotion and assignment to two Michigan cavalry regiments (he believed because of political machinations), now found himself commanding the entire Michigan Brigade recently attached to Judson Kilpatrick's division.

Armstrong may have been caught by surprise at his sudden promotion, but unprepared, never. That night, his orderly scrounged up two cloth stars that he quickly sewed on the collar of a blue, Navy shirt that Custer had procured earlier from a gunboat officer. Where the rest of his uniform, if you can call it that, came from is anyone's guess.

Captain James H. Kidd of the Sixth Michigan Cavalry, who met Custer for the first time on June 30, left us with an indelible portrait of the newly minted brigadier general:

> "Looking at him closely, this is what I saw: An officer superbly mounted who sat on his charger as if to the manor born. Tall, lithe, active, muscular, straight as an Indian and quick in his movements, he had the fair complexion of a school girl. He was clad in a suit of black velvet, elaborately trimmed with gold lace, which ran down the outer seams of his trousers, and almost covered the sleeves of his cavalry jacket, and a necktie of brilliant crimson was tied in a graceful knot at the throat, the long ends falling carelessly in front. The double rows of buttons on his breast were arranged in groups of

twos, indicating the rank of brigadier general. A soft, black hat with a wide brim adorned with a gilt cord, and rosette encircling a silver star, was worn turned down on one side giving him a rakish air. His golden hair fell in graceful luxuriance nearly or quite to his shoulders, and his upper lip was garnished with a blond mustache. A sword, gilt spurs and top boots completed his unique outfit."

The farm boys from Michigan didn't know what to make of their new commander and some began to refer to him as the "boy General of the Golden Lock." In a few weeks, the necks of those same troopers would begin to sprout crimson neckerchiefs.

Custer had always commanded from the front, pushing himself into the middle of the action, even when on detached duty as a junior staff officer. He now intended to command his brigade in the same way and he wanted his men to know that he shared their every danger. Later, when time permitted, he had an orderly ride beside him carrying his personal pennant, a blue and red swallowtail guidon with crossed white sabers. When time permitted, he organized a brigade band, which closely followed the rank and file. Whenever he ordered the band to strike up "Yankee Doodle Dandy," his men knew that action was imminent.

Custer and his Michigan troopers hardly had time to become acquainted when their relationship was put to the test. In the next week, Custer's brigade was thrown into action against Confederate Maj. Gen. J.E.B. Stuart's "Invincibles" in southern Pennsylvania at Hanover and Hunterstown as sideshow to that epic three-day clash between "Bobbie" Lee's Army of Northern Virginia and George "old snapping turtle" Meade's Army of the Potomac, known to us today as the Battle of Gettysburg.

A Quick Look at the Battle of Gettysburg

We don't feel that a lengthy rehash of the Battle of Gettysburg is really necessary for the Custer buff; however, those of you unfamiliar with this epic battle might appreciate a basic introduction to those momentous three days in July 1863. So, here is our brief synopsis.

On July 1, the first morning of the engagement, the vanguard of the Army of Northern Virginia, which had invaded Pennsylvania, and the Army of the Potomac attempting to shield major eastern cities, collided west of Gettysburg. The fighting increased in intensity throughout the day as more Union and Confederate troops reached the battlefield. By 4 p.m., Union troops were routed and retreated through Gettysburg. While many soldiers were captured, a large number took refuge in the town's cellars and basements. The remaining Union forces rallied south of the town on Cemetery and Culp's Hills, which they held through the night. By July 2, most major elements of both armies had arrived on the battlefield. Confederate commander, Gen. Robert E. Lee launched attacks against the Union left and right flanks to try and dislodge Gen. George Gordon Meade's army from its formidable position on Cemetery Ridge. Confederate Gen. James Longstreet made good progress in his attack, but was thwarted by Union reinforcements from the right and center. Gen. Richard Ewell's Second Corps ("Stonewall" Jackson's old command) was able to take part of Culp's Hill, but was thrown back in other areas. Heavy fighting took place in the center at positions named the Devil's Den, Rose's Wheatfield and Little Round Top, the latter hill being where Col. Joshua Chamberlain's 20th Maine infantrymen made their famous stand, capped by a bayonet charge.

On July 3, Ewell again tried to rout the Yankees from Culp's Hill, while Lee focused on the Union center. Following a two-hour bombardment, Lee deliberately sent 12,500 infantrymen across a three-quarter-mile-wide open field in a desperate effort to break the Union lines on Cemetery Ridge. This ruinous attack, later named Pickett's Charge after one of its three commanders, Maj. Gen. George Pickett, was beaten back with heavy losses, including Confederate Gen. Lewis Armistead, a pre-war friend of Union Gen. John Reynolds, who was fatally shot on the first day of the battle. The Civil War was truly a fratricidal war.

As Pickett's Charge was getting under way, Confederate cavalry under Gen. Wade Hampton was driven back by Federal cavalrymen, including Custer's Michigan Brigade, in a hard-fought battle east of town.

Suffering three days of heavy losses, Lee made the fateful decision over the night of July 3 to break off the fight and withdraw to Virginia. Casualties over the three days had been heavy, totaling approximately 50,000 for both sides. The Battle of Gettysburg is generally thought of as the high-water mark of the Confederacy, a defeat from which it never fully recovered.

In late June 1863, J.E.B. Stuart detached his command from Lee's army to undertake a reconnaissance-in-force by swinging his cavalrymen south and then east of the advancing Union Army. Meanwhile, Pleasonton's Cavalry Corps attempted to protect the Army of the Potomac's right flank. On June 30th, the two forces unexpectedly collided on the Littletown road south of Hanover, Pa. The skirmishing continued all that day with neither side gaining an advantage. Stuart broke off the fight at dusk, and then slipped around the Federals' left flank to continue his northward push the next day through Dover to Carlisle, Pa. Gen. Kilpatrick countered with a move north to East Berlin. The next day orders arrived from Meade calling for the concentration of Union forces at the town of Gettysburg where the main armies had just clashed. Meade's orders compelled Kilpatrick to backtrack through the village of Hunterstown, Pa. The two opposing cavalry forces collided again at about 4:30 in the afternoon just south of the village. The Confederates, some 1,750 strong, were commanded by Brig. Gen. Wade Hampton, a wealthy South Carolinian; they had never been beaten by Union cavalry. But, the tide of war, in so far as the cavalry was concerned, was about to turn. Unknown to Custer, his Michigan Brigade was about to do battle with Cobb's Legion, commanded by an old West Point friend, Georgian Pierce M. B. Young. They had parted at the Point two years before with words to the effect that the next time they met it would be on a battlefield, and so it came to be on a Pennsylvania country road south of Hunterstown.

In the midst of the fight, Custer's mount was shot from under him, leaving him afoot until rescued by one of his troopers. Armstrong had no time to reflect on his narrow escape because orders arrived ordering Gregg's division, of which the Michiganders were a part, to Two Taverns, just southeast of Gettysburg. En route, the Michigan Brigade received new orders to cover the Army's rear at the Hanover Road's intersection with another previously unheralded track known locally as "Low Dutch Road," some four miles east of Gettysburg.

If Custer's reputation as a cavalry commander had its beginning with the skirmish at Hunterstown, it became legendary in the battle at Rummel Farm on July 3. Custer realized that Brig. Gen. David McMurtrie Gregg's cavalry division, of which his command was a part, blocked the advance of Stuart's southerners tasked by Lee to find the rear of the Union Army at the same time that Maj. Gen. George Pickett led his division in its disastrous "charge" against the center of the Union line a few miles to the west.

Here, Armstrong gathered up his Seventh Michigan Regiment and rode to their front with the rallying cry, "Come on, you Wolverines!", he led them in a mounted charge that blunted the advance of the First Virginia Cavalry. Hours of cavalry charges and close-quarters combat ensued. Later, when Wade Hampton's troopers moved to counterattack, Custer joined Col. Charles H. Town, commander of the First Michigan, in blunting the attack, again shouting, "Come on, you Wolverines!", as his battle cry (aided, one must add, by a few well-placed Union artillery batteries.)

Custer's role in the turning back of Stuart, while a small event in the much larger battle, meant that Stuart's vaunted "Invincibles" played no role in the climatic struggle raging that day. Attesting to the fierceness of the cavalry action at Rummel Farm is the fact that the Michigan Brigade lost 257 men, the highest number of casualties in any cavalry brigade during the Battle of Gettysburg.

The Michigan Brigade then shadowed the Army of Northern Virginia as it moved south licking its wounds. All of Kilpatrick's division halted near Falmouth, Va., across the Rappahannock River from Fredericksburg, and it remained there until September 13 when it crossed the river to conduct a reconnaissance-in-force. During the fighting that ensued, Armstrong was unhorsed and wounded in the foot by shrapnel from an artillery shell. He parlayed his wound into a three-week furlough in Monroe, basking there in the glow the eastern press had conjured up around his name. It was during this furlough that Autie cemented his love relationship with Libbie Bacon that would lead to their marriage.

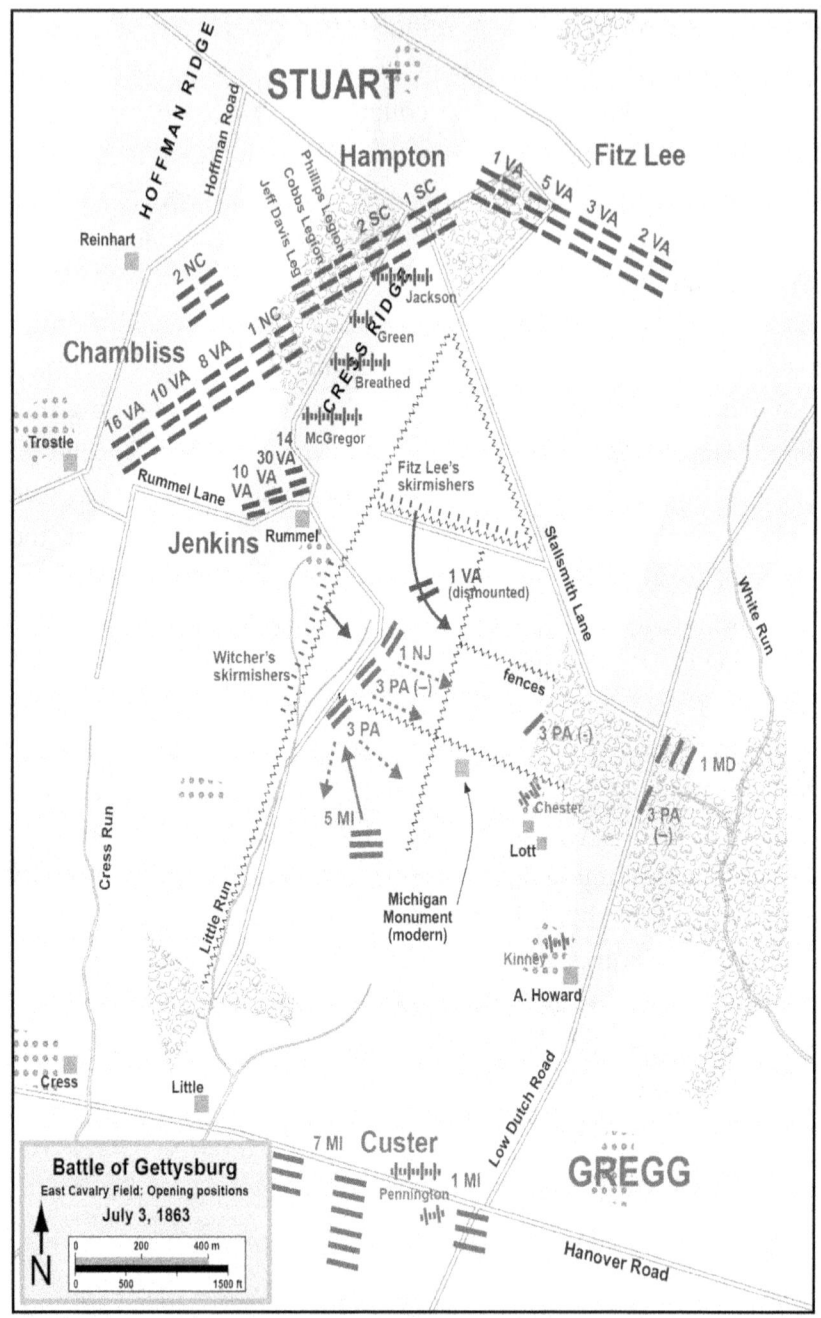

East Cavalry Field Battle Map (Hal Jesperson via Wikimedia)

Finding Custer Near Gettysburg

North Cavalry Field

The Hunterstown battlefield, which is also known as "North Cavalry Field," is privately owned and includes a power plant. The village of Hunterstown has a small plaque commemorating the nearby battlefield. On July 2, 2008, the town unveiled a marble monument dedicated to Custer.

East Cavalry Field

The battlefield where Custer and his Michigan Brigade fought has been preserved as part of the Gettysburg National Military Park known as the East Cavalry Battlefield Site. It is included as a non-numbered stop on the Self-Guiding Auto Tour. (You can pick up the brochure describing the complete tour at the Park Visitor Center.) The Site can be reached from the Gettysburg Town Square by driving east for four miles on York Road, which becomes Highway 116 (Hanover Road.)

An interior road runs past a monument dedicated to the Michigan Brigade, the inscription reads:

> This monument
> marks the field where the
> Michigan Cavalry Brigade
> under its gallant leader
> General George A. Custer
> rendered signal and distinguished
> service in assisting to defeat the
> further advance of a numerically
> superior force under the Confederate
> General J.E.B. Stuart, who in
> conjunction with Pickett's Charge
> upon the centre, attempted to turn
> the right flank of the Union

Army at that critical hour of
conflict upon the afternoon of
July 3rd 1863.
Field held from 8 a.m. until 7 p.m.

1st Mich. - Killed 10 men. Wounded 6 officers, 37 men. Missing 20 men.
5th Mich. - Killed 1 officer, 7 men. Wounded 1 officer, 29 men. Missing 18 men.
6th Mich. - Killed 1 man. Wounded 2 officers, 24 men. Missing 1 man.
7th Mich. - Killed 13 men. Wounded 4 officers, 44 men. Missing 39 men.
Total casualties 257.

Exploring the Gettysburg Battlefield

The echoes of this famous Civil War battle still resonate in this historic town in southern Pennsylvania. More than 2 million visitors each year head to the Gettysburg National Military Park — so many that National Park Service has recently made huge changes to accommodate the interest.

The Gettysburg National Battlefield Museum Foundation, partnering with the National Park Service, has rehabilitated large portions of the battlefield over the last 10 years, including removing outdated visitor facilities and parking lots from the Union battle line on Cemetery Ridge. It constructed a new museum and visitor facilities, rehabilitated portions of the battlefield and worked to preserve the Park's collection of Civil War archives and artifacts, including the iconic 19th century Cyclorama painting of Pickett's Charge.

The Park Service maintains that the new museum and visitor center allows the Park to better care for its collection of over 738,000 Civil War artifacts and archival items. An advisory committee of 11 historians assisted the foundation to develop new museum exhibits to enhance the visitor's experience. The improvements cost $95 million, which include some elements not in the initial estimates — a $10 million endowment to provide ongoing support for building maintenance and preservation of the collection. Enhancing all that effort, the National Park Service (www.nps.gov/gett) planted 13 peach orchards, working with the Friends of the National Parks at Gettysburg on this two-year project. Many of the Sherfy peach trees planted earlier in 1979 were declining or had already died; those trees were removed —roots and all — about 10 years ago. Before the new trees could be planted, however, a cover crop had be grown at the site for two years to rid the area of harmful nematodes, a parasitic worm that feeds on tree roots. The replanting worked and the new peach trees are thriving

The revitalization of other parts of the battlefield began a few years back as well, when the Park Service removed the massive commercial observation tower that loomed over the battlefield and that many visitors and purists viewed as an eyesore that did not contribute to an understanding of the battle. (The dismantled tower was sold for scrap to help to defray the cost of bringing it down. The Foundation also sold odd bits as souvenirs to help with the expense.) The results of all this work have been to greatly enhance the visitor's appreciation and understanding of this pivotal Civil War engagement.

The Gettysburg National Military Park is located in southwest Pennsylvania and can be most easily accessed from the south by leaving I-70 at Frederick, Md. from Exits 52 or 53 on to Highway 15 or from the north by taking Exit 236 off the Pennsylvania Turnpike at Harrisburg.

The Museum and Visitor Center are open daily from 8 a.m.

to 5 p.m. from November 1 through March 31; 8 a.m. to 6 p.m. from April 1 through October 31. They are closed Thanksgiving, Christmas and New Year's Day. Admission is charged that includes a film and the Cyclorama. National Park Passes are not accepted at the Museum and Visitor Center. The Soldier's National Cemetery, where Lincoln gave his famous "Gettysburg Address," is open from dawn to sundown to foot traffic only (except for the mobility impaired who need a special permit.) Be sure to pick up the free Self-Guiding Auto Tour guide at the Visitor Center. It will guide you around the battlefield to 16 numbered stops plus the Barlow Knoll Loop, historic downtown Gettysburg and the East Cavalry Battle Site.

Knowledgeable tour guides are available from $65 to $135 depending on the number of people in your party. Tours run two hours and must be reserved three days prior to your visit by calling 1(877)874-2478. Bus tours with guides are also available.

CUSTER AFTER GETTYSBURG

The war raged on another two years, despite the pivotal July 1863 Union victories at Gettysburg and Vicksburg. When the Cavalry Corps of the Army of the Potomac was reorganized after Gen. Ulysses S. Grant came east in March 1864 to take charge of the Virginia theater, Custer found himself under the command of Grant's dashing cavalry commander, Maj. Gen. Philip Sheridan. His prior benefactor, Alfred Pleasonton, was moved west in the shake-up. Quickly, "Little Phil," who had previously held both infantry and cavalry commands under Grant, came to appreciate the jewel he had in Armstrong Custer; their close relationship would last until Custer's death.

Custer as a Brevet Brigadier General (Wikimedia)

But, first things first. In February 1864, Autie took leave to marry his Libbie, Elizabeth Clift Bacon, who he had known since they were children, but only formerly introduced to (the prerequisite for formal courtship) 14 months prior to the wedding. Libbie's father, Judge Daniel S. Bacon, at first did not approve of his daughter marrying a blacksmith's son. However, he changed his mind after a heart-to-heart talk with his daughter and having received Autie's sincere letter asking for her hand. Of course, it must have helped settle his mind to know that the now famous Brig. Gen. Custer was to become his son-in-law. The wedding took place on Feb. 9, 1864 in Monroe's crowded First Presbyterian Church, which still stands today. Autie, his hair trimmed and attired in his dress uniform, stood next to a resplendent Libbie, clothed in a white silk gown, her veil held back by a ringlet of orange blossoms.

The newlyweds traveled east on their honeymoon with three other couples, making stops in Buffalo and Rochester, N.Y. to visit Libbie's relatives. Then, it was on to West Point (where Libbie brewed up a tempest when her husband learned that she had been kissed by an Academy professor), New York City and Washington. When Armstrong reported for duty at Stevensburg, Va., Libbie was right there with him, sharing quarters on the top floor of Clover Hill, a large home that had been commandeered for the brigade headquarters. Her move began a pattern that lasted the duration of their marriage — Libbie made every possible effort to be at her husband's side, or as close to it as feasible, wherever Autie was posted. We have no doubt that she would have ridden with him to the Little Bighorn if given the opportunity. From Autie's existing letters we know that they enjoyed an intense sexual relationship during these early years of their marriage. Back on duty, and now commanding the Third Cavalry Division under Sheridan, Custer led his cavalry forces into the Shenandoah Valley in the fall of 1864, where they faced and defeated the Confederates under Lt. Gen. Jubal Early.

Libbie and Autie (Photo: Wikimedia)

One plum that unexpectedly fell into their basket of victories during this campaign was the capture of Wade Hampton's supply train, however, as fate would have it, their own supply train was captured in return, including Autie's personal baggage, leading to the publication of some of his intimate correspondence with Libbie.

Custer's Division then fought in Grant's Overland Campaign at the Battles of the Wilderness and Yellow Tavern, and in the largest cavalry action of the war —Trevilian Station (June 11-12, 1864.)

When "Old Jube" moved up the Shenandoah Valley to threaten Washington, D.C. in the fall of 1864, Sheridan ordered his Army of the Shenandoah to pursue. The two forces clashed at the Third Battle of Winchester (Sept. 19) and Tom's Brook (Oct. 9), after which Custer's men were largely responsible for destroying Early's army during a counterattack at Cedar Creek (Oct. 19). His principal opponent during these engagements was an old West Point friend, Confederate General Thomas Rosser, who he would encounter again in the 1870s under more benign circumstances. (At Tom's Brook, Autie recovered a photograph of Libbie lost with his baggage at Trevilian Station and captured Rosser's dress uniform, which he wore around camp to the delight of his men.)

While on furlough in January 1865, Autie experienced a religious conversion while praying in Monroe's Presbyterian Church that led him to accept Jesus Christ as his personal savior. We will never know the depth of that conversion, but it must have pleased Libbie mightily, given her religious bent. It seems to have had little effect on Autie's propensity to use profanity or his love of gambling.

The Third Division next supported the infantry during the Siege of Petersburg, finally helping break the Confederate lines in April 1865. The division would again see action at Dinwiddie Court House, Five Forks and Waynesboro. During this time, Custer climbed the advancement ladder, being awarded brevet promotions to brigadier general and then, major general in the Regular Army on March 13, 1865.

Custer's cavalrymen helped block the Confederate retreat from Petersburg at the Battle of Sayler's Creek, three days before Lee's surrender at Appomattox Court House, and Custer was present at the surrender ceremony, although Gen. James Longstreet had refused to surrender to him earlier. As a gift for Libbie, Sheridan later presented Armstrong with the portable desk (that he purchased from its owner for $20) on which Grant had written out the agreement, signed later by the two commanders, which surrendered the Army of Northern Virginia, effectively ending the war.

INDIAN FIGHTER

THE KANSAS INTERLUDE, 1868-72

On May 23, 1865, Brevet Maj. Gen. George Armstrong Custer, sitting astride Don Juan, his then favorite mount, led his Third Cavalry Division down Washington's Pennsylvania Avenue in the grand review of the Army of the Potomac. As he approached the reviewing stand, Don Juan tossed his bit and, racing with his rider, his signature red neckerchief streaming behind him, shot past the presidential reviewing stand. At that moment, Armstrong could have ridden into history not only as one of the youngest, but also one of the most accomplished cavalry commanders in American military history. By biographer Robert Utley's reckoning, Custer's "... generalship combined audacity, courage, leadership, judgment, composure, and an uncanny instinct for the critical moment and the action it demanded. He pressed the enemy closely and doggedly, charged at the right moment, deployed his units with skill, and applied personal leadership where and when most needed." (*Cavalier in Buckskin*, Chapter 2.)

But duty beckoned. Soon after reviewing his Division for the final time a few days later, Autie and his Libbie boarded the train for Cairo, Illinois and then, a steamboat bound for New Orleans to join the command of Philip Sheridan. Gen. Grant had charged Sheridan with mopping up lingering Confederate resistance in Texas and preparing for a possible campaign against troops of the French Second Empire operating in Mexico. The Custers traveled up the Red River to Alexandria, La. where Custer took command of a motley group of state volunteers who

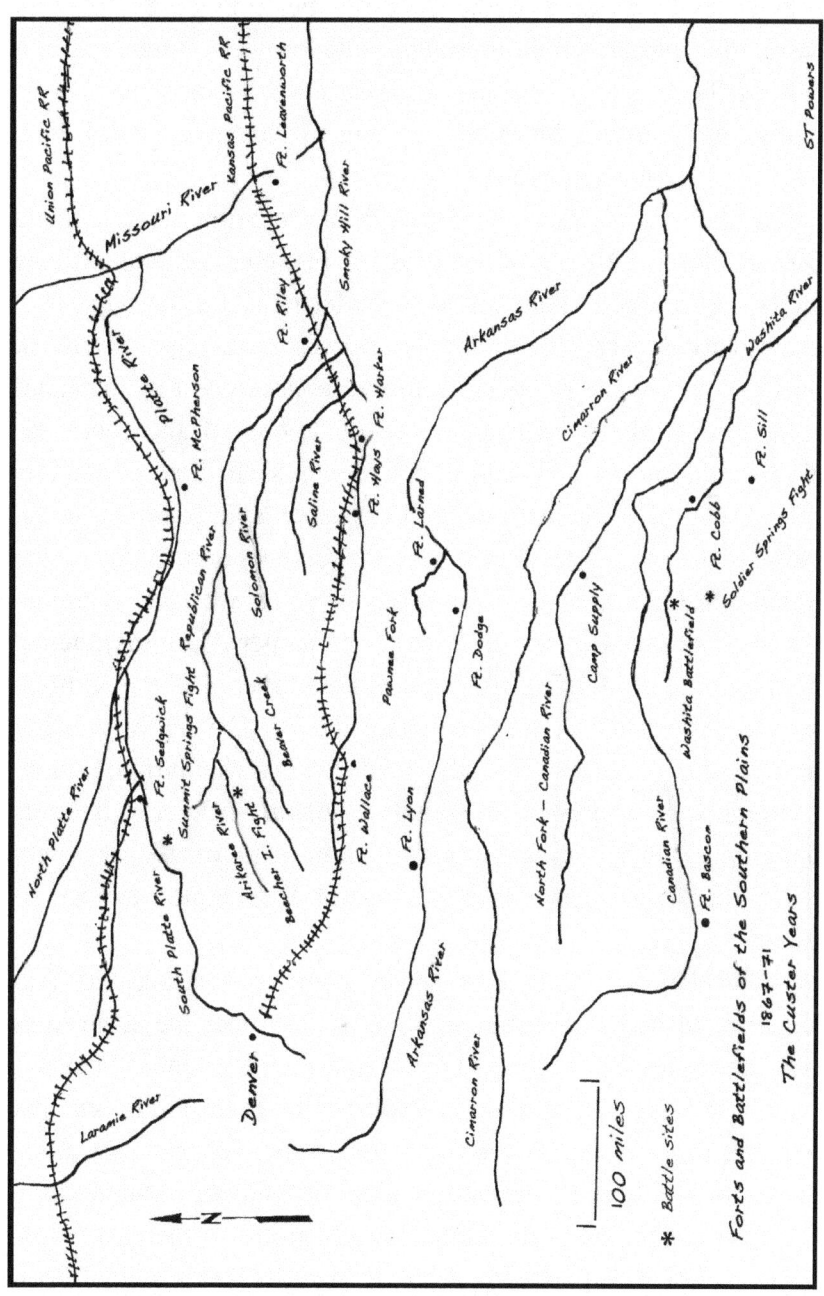

wanted no more of war or the United States Army, and were only interested in being discharged so they could return to their homes. There was friction from the beginning and Custer's harsh disciplinary measures did little to ease the tension. Eventually, Custer moved his headquarters to Hempstead, Texas, a town just north of Houston and later to Austin, a town Libbie described as "a pretty place."

In late December 1865, the War Department furloughed Custer, along with a number of other breveted general officers including George Crook and Wesley Merritt. After half a year of uncertainty during which Custer explored career opportunities in business and in the Mexican military, he accepted the lieutenant colonelcy of the 7th Cavalry Regiment, one of the four new cavalry regiments (7th-10th) that Congress had authorized in July 1866. He lacked the political clout and seniority to be awarded the colonelcy, but, since the titular commander of the Regiment, Col. Andrew J. Smith, was rarely with the regiment (he also commanded the District of the Upper Arkansas), actual field command fell to Custer. On October 16, the Custers arrived at Fort Riley, Kansas where the 7th Cavalry was being mustered in. They spent the next two weeks moving in to quarters that consisted of one-half of an officer's quarters building. Custer took temporary command of the regiment November 1, a week before leaving for Washington to face an examining board.

Fort Riley was one of seven Army posts that the War Department had established in Kansas to protect the stage lines that ran to the Colorado gold fields and now the Union Pacific's Eastern Division (the Kansas Pacific after 1869) railroad that was pushing its tracks westward toward Denver, roughly along the Smoky Hill River drainage. Fort Leavenworth, sited along the banks of the Missouri River lay 116 miles to the east, while Forts Harker, Hays and Wallace extended the Army's reach west almost to the border of the Colorado Territory. Forts Dodge and Larned constituted the southern outposts on the Arkansas River.

In the course of 1867, Armstrong, sometimes accompanied by Libbie, had reason to visit them all.

In Kansas, Custer was thrust into one of the Indian wars that had been raging all along the western frontier since the early 1860s. On the southern plains, outraged by the attack of Col. John Chivington's Third Regiment of Colorado Volunteers on the camps of Black Kettle and White Antelope at Sand Creek, Colo. Territory in November 1864, Cheyenne and Arapaho war parties interdicted traffic along the Platte and Smoky Hill trails, going so far as to first attack and then, burn Julesburg, Colo. in January 1865.

Settlers couldn't expect much help from the U.S. Army until the defeat of the Confederacy and its post-war reorganization. During the winter of 1866-67, Gen. Sheridan, now in command of the Military Division of the Missouri, determined on a military campaign against the warring tribes to force them to cease their raids and to confine themselves to various reservations that had been carved out for them on the southwestern plains. Sheridan gave tactical command of this punitive force to Gen. Winfield S. Hancock, a highly competent officer whose men had blunted Pickett's Charge at the Battle of Gettysburg. Eleven companies of Custer's 7th Cavalry Regiment became part of Hancock's 1,400-man force of cavalry, infantry and artillery.

Unfortunately, neither Hancock nor Custer had any experience in fighting Indians and that fact became painfully obvious during their 1867 campaign. Hancock moved his army south from Fort Riley in March and arrived at Fort Larned on April 7. His plan was apparently to overawe the chiefs of several bands of Cheyenne, Arapaho, Kiowa and Sioux camped about 30 miles upstream on the Pawnee Fork. Hancock first met with a handful of chiefs willing to come to the Fort, but, when he moved his force upriver, he was met by a line of Sioux and Cheyenne warriors barring his way. From Custer's account of this confrontation, this must have been the first time he had encountered a large number of Plains Indian warriors attired in full battle regalia. He described it years later as "one of the finest and most imposing military displays ... which it has ever been my lot to behold. ... Most of the Indians were mounted; all were bedecked in their brightest colors, their heads crowned with the brilliant war bonnet, their lances bearing the crimson pennant, bows strung, and quivers full of barbed arrows."

Fortunately, Indian Agents Edward Wynkoop and Jesse Leavenworth, traveling with Hancock, managed to convince the Indians of his peaceful intent, but, when he later encamped near their villages that evening, the Indians decided to slip away during the night. Informed of their intentions by his native scouts, Hancock ordered Custer to surround the camp with the 7th Cavalry to prevent their escape. At dawn, much to his chagrin, Armstrong found the camp deserted, tipis still standing, except for an old woman and a young half-breed girl. An angry Hancock unwisely ordered Custer and eight troops of the 7th to pursue the fleeing Indians. (While out alone buffalo hunting during this chase, Armstrong managed to shoot his own horse [Libbie's favorite] in the head, yet survive the mishap uninjured.) His command followed the ever-diminishing trail north until it reached the Smoky Hill Trail, where the troopers found that the Lookout stage station had been burned and its employees massacred. Then, after burying the dead and running low on provisions, Custer turned his command east to Fort Hays where he expected to be resupplied.

Meanwhile, Hancock, despite the protests of Wynkoop and Leavenworth, burned the abandoned village, both tipis and personal belongings, before retiring to Fort Leavenworth, one would assume to brood over his failed campaign. His destruction of the village helped ignite a summer marked by violence, with war parties raiding all along the western trails. In the fall, Hancock was relieved of his command.

Custer, having pushed his men and horses to cover 150 miles in four days, found himself stuck in Fort Hays because of a lack of forage and provisions brought about by flooded streams farther east. He established a camp on Big Creek about a half-mile from Fort Hays where Libbie joined him in May for a two-week visit.

Custer, now resupplied, took the field again on June 1, riding north to Fort McPherson where he met briefly with General Sherman. He then moved west, arriving at Fort Wallace on the 13th, covering 181 miles in a week. (Custer was always willing to push himself to the limit, but many of his men were not and they deserted his command in large numbers throughout his time in Kansas.) Now uncertain of Libbie's whereabouts and worried about the cholera epidemic sweeping through Kansas settlements and military posts, Armstrong abandoned his command and, with an escort of troopers, rode through Fort Hayes, reaching Fort Harker on June 19, whereupon he boarded a Kansas Pacific train for Fort Riley where Libbie was safely ensconced.

That scamper across central Kansas and his alleged treatment of deserters earlier that summer led to his court martial and conviction on three of the charges that had been brought. The court ordered him suspended from the Army for a year, with the forfeiture of pay. Hardly chastised, Autie and Libbie enjoyed Sheridan's quarters at Fort Leavenworth over the winter of 1867-68, later returning to Monroe to visit relatives.

Indian raids and futile Army campaigns continued through 1868 while frustration mounted in the Army high command. Congress had created a peace commission in 1867 that met with the leading chiefs on Medicine Lodge Creek in southern Kansas that fall to persuade them to move their bands onto designated reservations in the Indian Territory. Later that fall, a separate peace commission met with the Sioux at Fort Laramie in an effort to persuade the various sub-tribes to accept a large reservation spanning most of present day South Dakota west of the Missouri River. Although treaties were duly signed, the effort proved futile; neither white settlers nor Indians were prepared to abide by their provisions.

THE BATTLE OF THE WASHITA, NOVEMBER 27, 1868 AND ITS AFTERMATH

By the fall of 1868, Gen. Sheridan, who believed that only a successful military campaign would bring about the subjugation of the tribes, had decided on a winter campaign and, with Sherman's concurrence, convinced the War Department to recall Custer to active duty before his suspension had ended. Custer hesitated not a moment, leaving Monroe for Kansas before official confirmation of his recall had arrived. He was in Leavenworth on September 30 and shortly thereafter, met with Sheridan at Fort Hays. By October 11, he had joined his regiment on Cavalry Creek, 42 miles south of Fort Dodge, Kan., but soon moved his command back to Fort Dodge because of supply problems. There, in an orgy of activity, he organized an elite company of sharpshooters after a marksmanship competition and remounted each troop on horses of a like color in hopes of improving morale. On November 1, Sheridan ordered veteran Indian fighter Gen. Alfred Sully and Custer to establish an advance base on the North Canadian River that became known as Camp Supply. The 7th Cavalry left Fort Dodge on the twelfth and reached the Camp Supply site five days later. Sheridan arrived on Nov. 21. At that time, Sully returned to Fort Harker because his jurisdiction did not extend as far south as Camp Supply. (In addition, he didn't enjoy Sheridan's confidence after he had earlier led a desultory scouting patrol.) That move also simplified the chain of command, Sheridan

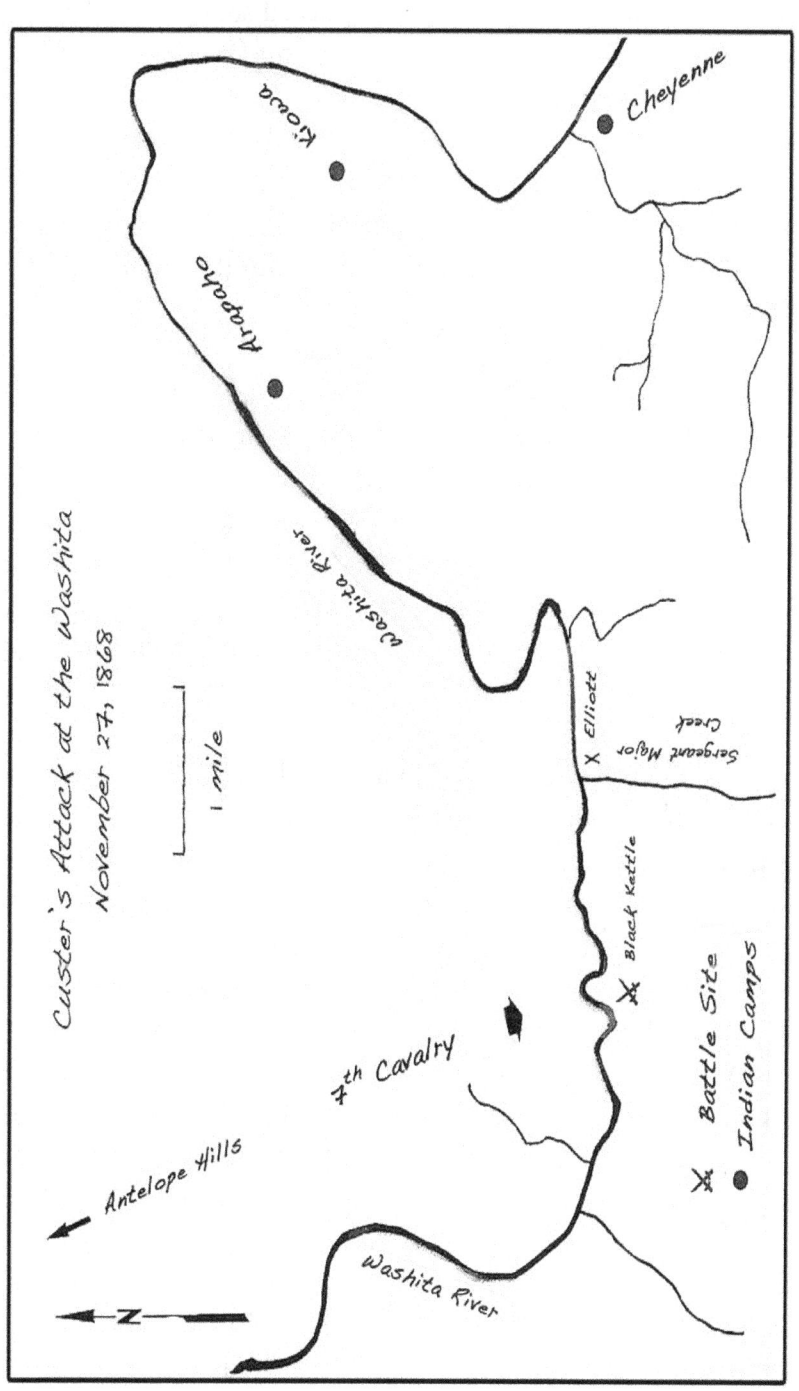

quickly issued orders to Custer "to proceed south in the direction of the Antelope Hills, thence toward the Washita River, the supposed winter seat of the hostile tribes, to destroy their villages and ponies, to kill or hang all warriors, and bring back all women and children." Sheridan also sent two other Army columns, one marching from Fort Lyon, Colorado Territory and the other from Fort Bascom, New Mexico Territory, toward the South Canadian River as blocking forces.

The 7th Cavalry, better than 900 strong in a column four abreast, rode out of Camp Supply in the early morning of November 23 in a blizzard, with the regimental band bravely playing "The Girl I Left Behind Me." Sheridan and Custer had not waited for the arrival of the newly recruited 19th Regiment of Kansas Volunteers, which was at that moment struggling through the breaks of the Cimarron River to the north. For the next four days the column, preceded by a contingent of scouts and trailed by wagons, struggled south through a foot of snow following compass directions in order to locate the Antelope Hills, just north of the valley of the Washita. By the 25th, the column had reached the South Canadian River without having encountered any Indians or Indian signs, whereupon Custer detached his second in command, Maj. Joel H. Elliott, with three troops to scout up the north bank. The remaining troopers then crossed the swollen river, double-teaming the wagons. Jack Corbin, one of the scouts, soon brought the news that Elliott had cut a large Indian trail heading southeast. Custer ordered Corbin back with orders for Elliott to follow the trail and then, led the main column southeast in an effort to find the trail, assumed to be that of a large war party headed back to its winter camp. When Custer intercepted Elliott's trail near dark on the 26th, he sent a rider forward to tell Elliott to halt in place in order to feed his men and horses and await his arrival. The two columns joined up around 9:00 p.m. and began a silent advance through the crusty snow toward the Antelope Hills and the Washita valley.

About midnight the regiment reached the river, and then turned downstream. The leader of the Osage scouts, Little Beaver, soon rode in saying that he smelled smoke. After further scouting the valley, Little Beaver returned, replying to Custer inquiry: "Heap Injuns down there." It was not the last time in his supercharged career that Custer would hear similar words.

Not wanting to alert the Indian camp of his presence and allow it to slip away, Custer quickly made a number of tactical decisions based on his scanty information. He split his command into four divisions, ordered the troopers to cache their packs where their horses stood and the divisions to move into positions that would allow them to attack the camp from four directions at dawn. The wagon train with its escort, plodding along in the rear, was left to take care of itself.

The Indian camp of 51 lodges, located in a shallow bend on the south side of the Washita, was that of Black Kettle, the peacefully inclined Cheyenne chief whose same camp had been attacked almost exactly four years before at Sand Creek in the Colorado Territory. Black Kettle had recently returned from Fort Cobb, Okla. after Col. William B. Hazen had rebuffed his efforts to secure protection. Citing the recent raids into Kansas by Cheyenne war parties, Hazen denied Black Kettle's request.

Just after first light, as Custer was about to order the band to strike up "Gary Owen," the regimental marching song and signal for the coordinated attack, a shot rang out. Not wanting to lose the element of surprise, he ordered the four troops under his direct command, the sharpshooters and scouts to attack directly across the river into the camp. The attack was anything but coordinated, but it was none-the-less successful. Custer later wrote: "There was never a more complete surprise." Cheyenne warriors, some undoubtedly just returned from their raid into Kansas, put up a stout resistance, retreating to the river, where the banks provided them with firing positions. Black Kettle was not so fortunate; he and his wife were shot from the saddle as they attempted to flee the camp. Lt. Louis M. Hamilton, grandson of Alexander Hamilton, fell early in the fight; Capt. Albert Barnitz was gut shot, but survived his wound. As the fighting continued through the morning, Custer received a report from Lt. Edward Godfrey that his scouting party had seen large Indian camps downstream and mounted warriors riding toward Black Kettle's camp. Custer at first scoffed at Godfrey's report, but soon large numbers of warriors appeared and began to probe his lines. For the remainder of the afternoon, the dismounted troopers occupied themselves with burning the tepees and their contents and slaughtering the camp's pony herd, over 800 animals. Indian efforts to infiltrate the 7th's lines were met with local counterattacks. One of Armstrong's nagging concerns was the fate of Maj. Elliott and the 19 troopers who earlier had ridden off with him at dawn in pursuit of Indians fleeing the camp. A scouting party later sent downstream for two miles had been unable to make contact with Elliott or ascertain his situation. At this time Armstrong made a command decision to abandon Elliott and his men to their fate in order to extricate his regiment from its perilous position. Just before dusk, he formed up his troops and, with band playing, began to advance downstream toward the other Indian camps. Warriors who had been harassing his perimeter now galloped away to protect their villages. As night fell, Custer reversed direction and led his men north out of the Washita valley. The regiment continued on horseback until 2 a.m. when it halted for a short rest period. At 10 a.m. on the 28th they reached the wagon train, which the Indians had failed to find, and dismounted for a well-earned breakfast.

Custer sent word ahead to Sheridan at Camp Supply of his victory, saying that "We have cleaned Black Kettle and his band out so thoroughly that they can neither fight, dress, sleep, eat or ride without sponging on their friends." He rode into Camp Supply led by his Osage scouts, painted for war, his civilian scouts and prisoners. Next came the regimental band playing "Gary Owen" and then the sharpshooters, all followed by a buckskin-clad Armstrong and the 7th Cavalry in a long column of fours. Sheridan and his officers, the officers and men of the 19th Kansas Cavalry, who had finally arrived, stood in review as this victorious cavalcade passed. It was a triumphant occasion for Armstrong and he made the most of it.

Hidden behind all this pomp was the final casualty list for the regiment: two officers and 19 troopers killed and 14 others wounded. Included in the list of dead were Maj. Elliott and the 19 troopers who had followed him in pursuit of fleeing Cheyenne; the detachment was ambushed, killed and the dead mutilated. Estimates of Cheyenne losses, including warriors, women and children, ranged from 31 to 103. Fifty-three women and children were taken captive.

For Sheridan, the attack at the Washita was only the opening move in his winter campaign. He had already detached two other columns across the southern plains and he didn't intend for the cavalry at Camp Supply to remain idle. Hardly giving the 7th time to resupply, and despite blizzard conditions, he ordered the 7th back to the Washita battlefield where they discovered the butchered bodies of Maj. Elliott and his men. On December 12, the column, now some 1,500 in number, moved down the Washita, following an Indian trail that led to Fort Cobb, Indian Territory. Here, Sheridan and Custer were confronted by Gen. William B. Hazen who, speaking in his capacity as Indian Agent, maintained that Chief Satanta's (Set'tainte : White Bear) Kiowas camped nearby were friendly and under his protection. Sheridan thought Hazen's assertions were a "pretty good joke," but eventually backed down.

Early in 1869, the Indians and soldiers camped near Fort Cobb exhausted the local food and forage resources prompting Sheridan to move everyone south 30 miles to a spot at the foot of the Wichita Mountains that he named Fort Sill in honor of Brig.

Gen. Joshua W. Sill, a West Point classmate who fell in the Civil War.

Another of Sheridan's columns under Maj. Andrew W. Evans, marching from Fort Bascom, had attacked a Comanche camp at Soldier Spring on Christmas Day 1868, routing the defenders after a two-day battle and burning the entire camp. Maj. Eugene A. Carr commanded the Fort Lyon column, consisting of elements of the 5th and 10th Cavalry Regiments that marched on December 2, and then moved southeast to the North Canadian. One of Carr's scouts was William Cody, later to become internationally famous as "Buffalo Bill" Cody. These two columns were meant to keep the wandering bands from fleeing to the west. Evans was at least successful in bringing a Comanche band to battle, but Carr had nothing to show for his arduous winter march. Carr's chance came the next summer when his command was ordered from Fort McPherson to campaign in western Kansas and eastern Colorado. In July 1869, Carr's force, again employing the services of Cody, surprised Tall Bull's Cheyenne camp at Summit Springs in the South Platte valley, routing the Indians in a fight that ended with the death of Tall Bull.

In the meantime, Custer moved west from Fort Sill in March, managing to locate a Cheyenne village on Sweetwater Creek in the Texas Panhandle. Instead of striking the village as he had done on the Washita, Custer parlayed with the Cheyenne chiefs in an attempt to secure the release of two white women being held captive. When his efforts proved unsuccessful, he seized three of the chiefs, whereupon the Cheyenne then gave up the women. Custer held the chiefs as prisoners, but promised to release them and the Washita prisoners, then being held at Fort Hays, when the bands came into their reservations in the spring. Now, virtually out of provisions, Armstrong led his ragtag column back to Camp Supply and then to Fort Hays where it arrived on April 6. Fully two-thirds of his 800 men were by then dismounted, with their dead horses marking the long trail home. The 1868-69 winter campaign was finally over. There were too many partial successes and enough outright failures to deem it a success, but it had demonstrated that the regulars could operate against the hostile tribes in the depths of a nasty winter.

By then, Phil Sheridan had long since departed the Kansas plains for Washington, where Gen. Ulysses S. Grant, now President Grant, appointed him Lt. Gen. of the Army, second in command to Gen. Sherman, now Commanding General of the Army.

The summer of 1869 was quieter than the previous four with the exception of the fight at Summit Springs. The 7th Cavalry occupied itself with policing the Kansas Pacific Railroad as it continued to build west toward Denver. Armstrong hoped to be appointed to the command of the 7th when that position became vacant due to the retirement of Col. Smith, but was again passed over this time in favor of Col. Samuel D. Sturgis. He then applied for the vacant post of Superintendent of West Point, to be again passed over in favor of Lt. Col. Emory Upton.

Autie and Libbie spent that summer in a tent camp near Fort Hays. The 7th Cavalry was bivouacked nearby at a location dubbed Camp Sturgis, after its new commander. Armstrong occasionally led his troopers on excursion along the Smoky Hill River trail and entertained a number of visiting dignitaries and politicians who wanted him to guide them on buffalo hunts. Apparently, that mishap in 1867, when he had accidently shot the horse he was riding, had not dampened his ardor for the chase. In October, the Custers moved to Fort Leavenworth. Later, Armstrong traveled to the Midwest, but both he and Libbie were back at Leavenworth in January 1870.

The summer of 1870 proved to be another bloody one, with the 7th Cavalry operating out of Forts Hays and Harker to protect the Kansas Pacific Railroad and the settlements it had spawned. For a good part of the summer the Custers remained at Camp

Sturgis. Custer personally led a sweep along the Saline River in July, but the Indian raiding parties were undeterred. It would take another determined campaign by converging Army columns in 1874-75, the Red River War, to force the southern tribes onto their assigned reservations.

The Custers spent the first part of the winter of 1870-71 at Fort Leavenworth. Then, the Army granted Armstrong's request for a 60-day furlough to pursue business opportunities in New York; he and Libbie boarded the train for their trip back East on January 11, 1871. The Army eventually extended Armstrong's furlough for another six months and, by the time it ended on September 3, 1871, the 7th Cavalry had been transferred from the Kansas frontier to the upper South for Reconstruction duty. Armstrong's new headquarters were located in Louisville, Kentucky and he and Libbie soon took up residence in an old hotel in Elizabethtown, 40 miles to the south, a dull town according to Libbie. The troops of the 7th Cavalry were scattered throughout the South.

Armstrong saw the Kansas plains only once again in January 1872 when he staged a buffalo hunt, complete with reservation Sioux and "Buffalo Bill" Cody, for the Grand Duke Alexis of Russia. Even Gen. Sheridan, who had arranged the excursion, tagged along to enjoy the fun. That hunt made headlines all over the nation. When it was over and Alexis had collected his buffalo, the party rode the Union Pacific west to Cheyenne and there entrained for Denver, where throngs of Coloradans greeted their arrival, hoping to catch a glimpse of the famous entourage. Both Custers later accepted the Grand Duke's invitation to travel as his guests down the Mississippi River to New Orleans where Alexis served as honorary Grand Marshal in the 1872 Mardi Gras parade.

Armstrong and Alexis kept in touch until the former's death at the Little Bighorn. The Grand Duke later sent Libbie $500 in her husband's memory.

Finding Custer in Texas and Nebraska

We have chosen to place information on the various U.S. Army forts where Armstrong and Libbie either resided or visited from 1867 to 1876, along with information on the Washita Battlefield National Monument, in Appendix 1. However, there are other widely scattered sites associated with the Custers after the Civil War that deserve mention as well. These we have listed by state.

Texas:

When Custer's command moved to Hempstead, Tex. in 1865, they camped on the Liendo Plantation. The Plantation's owner, Leonard Walker Groce had been an ardent supporter of the Confederacy during the war, sending his four sons off to fight and allowing his plantation grounds to be used for as a military camp. At first Libbie refused Groce's offer to let her quarter in the plantation house, but when she later fell ill, she relented and moved to more comfortable quarters until she had recovered. Armstrong enjoyed hunting with Groce and his friends, even to the point of accepting a gift of five hounds from his host. One suspects that Armstrong's lifelong affection for hunting dogs began here; he was never without them for the rest of his life. When he left Hempstead for Austin in November of 1865, he gave instructions that Groce's property rights were to be respected by Union officials.

The Groce plantation at Hempstead still stands and, although now the private property of the Detering family, is open to tourists on the first Saturday of each month. There is a Civil War reenactment at the plantation at the end of November. A marker at the entrance notes the residency of the Custers.

In Austin, Custer made his headquarters in an abandoned home for the blind located on the outskirts of the town. That building has been preserved as part of the University of Texas campus as the Arno Nowotny building, the offices of the Dolph Briscoe Center of American History. The building stands at the corner of East Martin Luther King Boulevard and Red River Street on the east side of the campus. It is open on weekdays from 8:00 a.m. to 5:00 p.m. There is no admission charge and there is metered parking nearby.

The cavalry bivouac was located in what is now Pease Park, west of the UT campus, off Martin Luther King Boulevard.

A few soldiers who were under Custer's command are buried in Oakwood Cemetery, Austin's oldest, located at 1601 Navasota St.

Nebraska:

Aside from Fort McPherson that we mention in Appendix 1, the only other Custer site of interest in Nebraska is a marker commemorating the buffalo hunt with Crown Prince Alexis located about ten miles from Hayes Center, Neb., and a few miles from the site of the hunting camp. There is also a marker on the actual site of the camp, but it is located on private land. Hayes Center is in a relatively remote area of southwest Nebraska that can be reached by leaving I-80 at Exit 158, 20 miles west of North Platte, and then driving 48 miles south to Hayes Center. During the last week in September of some years, reenactors stage a Grand Duke Alexis Rendezvous, where they reprise what has been called the last great buffalo hunt of the American West. The last Rendezvous was held on Sept. 18-20, 2015, with author and western-forts-authority Jeff Barnes giving the keynote talk. For information on a future Rendezvous contact the Lincoln County Historical Museum (2403 N. Buffalo Ave., North Platte, Neb.) at: Phone: (308) 534-5640 www.lincolncountymuseum.org/ or additional information is available at www.granddukealexis.com.

Custer's Engagements – Washita and Little Bighorn Rivers

It is impossible to resist the temptation to compare these two clashes between Lt. Col. George A. Custer's 7th Cavalry and the Cheyenne and Sioux nations, among the most warlike of the Plains Indian tribes. These fights, although separated by hundreds of miles and eight years in time, bear striking similarities. Both were precipitated by 7th Cavalry attacks on Indian camps that were thought to be hostile or harboring warriors hostile to American interests. In each attack, Custer hoped to achieve tactical surprise and was successful at the Washita. Yet, even the results of that victory were temporary at best, while, as we all know, his attack at the Little Bighorn ended disastrously in his death and the annihilation of his battalion. Paradoxically, the Sioux and Cheyenne's victory over Custer at the Little Bighorn proved ephemeral as well. Within a few years, harried by the Army and confronted with the near extinction of the vast buffalo herds on which their way of life depended, the last wandering bands were forced to give up their nomadic life for a sedentary existence on reservations assigned them by the federal government.

Both campaigns have other striking military similarities: originally both were conceived of winter campaigns aimed at convincing hostile bands to give up their resistance to further penetration by white, God-fearing Americans across the southern Plains and into the lush mountain valleys of the Dakota and

Montana Territories. The Army's strategy was to send multiple, converging columns against winter-bound Indian encampments that were most vulnerable during those months when there was little forage for the pony herds. Nor did the Indians believe that the U.S. Army would itself be capable of mounting winter campaigns because it faced equally great logistical problems, thus increasing the potential for surprise. Both Gens. Sherman and Sheridan consistently advocated a hardline policy toward recalcitrant Indian bands and implemented it whenever they could while they held positions of command in the 1860s and '70s. Only problems with command, logistics and the weather delayed the desired winter 1876 campaign until the late spring and early summer.

Even the more compassionate Americans, mostly easterners, who deplored using force against the western tribes never understood, sympathized with or wished to preserve the Indian culture. The only solutions they could conceive of to the problems presented by these indigenous peoples were to convince them peacefully into becoming dutiful Christian, subsistence farmers, while helping them along the path to cultural annihilation with minimal food and money subsidies. If mercifully those solutions did not call for physical eradication, they were certainly aimed at snuffing out the Indians' cultural and spiritual life.

Thus, as Custer paused his column in the Wolf mountains, on the divide between the Rosebud and the Little Bighorn, just past noon on June 25, 1876, he had fully expected to duplicate the tactics he had employed in his attack on Black Kettle's camp at the Washita eight years before — a surprise attack from multiple directions aimed at destroying the camp, driving off its defenders, capturing the pony herd while taking the women and children prisoners. The end result would be to force the free-roaming bands onto their designated reservations allowing vast tracks of land to be opened to white settlement.

In both campaigns, Custer launched mounted attacks with inadequate reconnaissance, banking on surprise and shock to carry the day. He was more concerned with the Indians slipping away, as they had done on the Pawnee Fork during Gen. Winfield S. Hancock's 1867 campaign, than he was with the warriors standing their ground in a bitter fight to the death. He gave up his plan for a dawn attack on June 26 because of warnings from his Indian scouts that his column had been detected. Thus, Maj. Marcus Reno's 174 troopers and scouts did not charge the Indian camp circles at first light on the 26th, as Custer had planned, but rather began their attack at around 3:10 in the afternoon of the 25th. Apparently taken by surprise by Reno's sudden appearance, the Indians recovered quickly enough first to stop Reno and then force his men into a panicked retreat.

Custer's dawn attack at the Washita had prevailed because he achieved tactical surprise, the size of his force (800 troopers) and the size (51 lodges) along with the relative isolation of Black Kettle's camp. (See our account in Chapter 3.) At the Little Bighorn, he found his command (647 officers, troopers, Indian auxiliaries and civilians) vastly outnumbered by warriors who had been assured of victory by Sitting Bull at a recent sun-dance ceremony and who would fight fanatically in the belief that defeat here meant the end of their independent, free-roaming life.

It is not the intent of the authors to delve deeply into the 139-year-old controversy over the fate the 209 men who rode north with Custer along the bluffs of the Little Bighorn, i.e., whether they fought bravely to the end or whether they succumbed to panic and were slaughtered in small groups that offered little resistance to the overwhelming numbers of Sioux and Cheyenne warriors. The readers will have to weigh the abundance of relevant arguments, especially those based on recent archaeological and historical investigations, and come to their own conclusions. But, let it be said, that if Custer had heeded the warnings of his Indian scouts as to the size and temper of the Indian camps on the Little Bighorn or had he known of the determined resistance mounted by Sioux and Cheyenne warriors against Crook's column on the Rosebud eight days before, he might have organized his attack differently on the 25th. But, Custer's ignorance of the true situation confronting him, Major Marcus Reno's retreat to the bluffs on the east side of the Little Bighorn, Capt. Frederick Benteen's tardiness in joining the fight and launching his attack with a green, under-strength regiment, divided into four non-supporting battalion — all contributed to the final disaster on Custer Hill.

ON TO MONTANA

THE YELLOWSTONE EXPEDITION, 1873

The advance of the Northern Pacific Railroad from Duluth, Minn., across the Dakota Territory and beyond brought the 7th Cavalry out of its role of policing the ex-Confederate States back onto the northern plains. Writing to Gen. Sheridan, Army Chief William T. Sherman noted that the "Indians will be hostile in an extreme degree, yet I think our interest is to favor the undertaking of the Road, as it will help to bring the Indian problem to a final solution." Accordingly, in 1873, the War Department canceled orders for the movement of the 7th to Louisiana and instead ordered the scattered troops of the regiment to assemble at Memphis for movement to their new temporary base at Fort Rice in the Dakota Territory. This would be the first time since its inception at Fort Riley in 1867 that the entire 7th Cavalry Regiment had been brought together, although it would be soon scattered again in the Dakota Territory.

The long march north began at Yankton, Dakota Territory and proceeded up the east side of the Missouri River. Libbie Custer and Maggie Calhoun, as privileged officers' wives, accompanied the march with their husbands, while the other wives moved up the Missouri by steamer. Libbie was most struck by the demoralized reservation Indians she encountered as well as the number of "rattle-snakes" infesting their campsites. Since there were no accommodations for wives at Fort Rice, they all soon departed on the Northern Pacific Railroad for homes back east. Libbie and Maggie temporarily moved in with their Monroe in-laws.

Fort Abraham Lincoln, an infantry post established the year before, was now designated as the new home for the 7th, but it required major additions before it could serve as a cavalry base. While the work was underway, the 7th took the field with the bulk of the regiment under Maj. David S. Stanley moving west along the Yellowstone River valley to protect Northern Pacific surveying parties. Two troops under Maj. Marcus Reno accompanied another party that was surveying the boundary with Canada.

The Stanley expedition, some 1,500 strong, left Fort Rice on June 20, 1873 and reached the Yellowstone River in late July, where it was met the steamboats *Far West* and *Josephine* bringing up supplies. On the march, an often-tipsy Stanley clashed with Armstrong, at one point ordering his subordinate arrested and banished to the rear of the column. Armstrong, it seems, had ridden ahead on a scouting foray without bothering to inform his commander. The next day a sober Stanley apologized. Thereafter, Stanley often lost in an alcoholic haze, left Armstrong to his own devices. So, Armstrong scouted, hunted and hobnobbed as he pleased with Tom Rosser, an old West Point classmate, ex-Confederate General and Civil War foe who was now chief engineer for the Northern Pacific.

The expedition established a temporary supply base above the mouth of Glendive Creek that became known as Stanley's Stockade. Leaving the infantry companies to guard the depot, Stanley and Custer scouted up river with about 90 men. Soon, Bloody Knife, Custer's favorite Arikara (Ree) scout, discovered a sign of a Sioux war party and warned them of the danger. Almost on cue, on August 4, while the column was resting in the shade of cottonwoods at the base of a long hill running parallel to the river, across from the mouth of the Tongue River, the Sioux struck. A small party of warriors lured Custer and a handful of troopers into a stern chase, but were not clever enough to spring the trap. Brother Capt. Tom Custer formed his troops into a dismounted skirmish line and, as his brother Armstrong and orderly passed through the line, fired on their Indian pursuers. Volleys broke the charge and after fending off warriors attacking on foot through the tall grass for several hours, Lt. Myles Moylan arrived with reinforcements convincing the Sioux to end the fight. The cavalry suffered only one man wounded, but sometime that day Sioux warriors fell on a small, detached party, killing regimental veterinarian Dr. John Honsinger, sutler Augustus Baliran and a trooper escorting them.

Stanley's column continued westward along the Yellowstone valley, one must assume in a more cautious manner, until it found Sitting Bull's campsite from which the warriors had attacked them on Aug. 8. At that point Stanley released Custer with eight troops on a night pursuit of the fleeing village. Some 36 hours later, the exhausted command found the spot near the mouth of the Bighorn River where the Indian camp had crossed to the south bank. The troopers tried to cross after them, but failed after several attempts. At dawn on the 11th, Sioux warriors gathered on the far bank and began firing across the river at the cavalrymen hoping to pin them down while their mounted brethren forded the river in flanking attacks. Custer countered by posting sharpshooters to answer the fire from across the river and sending out flanking companies to counter the mounted threat. Capt. Verling K. Hart, who led two companies upriver, then posted 20 men under Lt. Charles Braden on a point of elevated bench-land. Almost immediately, Braden's weak skirmish line came under attack from several hundred mounted warriors, but it managed to repulse them four times despite Braden himself being seriously wounded. Armstrong mounted the remainder of his command and, with the band striking up the familiar "Gary Owen," struck back at the Indians. Shortly thereafter, Stanley's column arrived on the scene (one assumes with its commander reasonably sober) from down river, releasing Capt. Thomas French's two companies to join Custer in pursuing the warriors, who had retreated back across the river, for eight miles before giving up the chase. Meanwhile, Stanley unlimbered his artillery pieces (probably 3" Ordnance Rifles, not actual heavy-caliber "Rodman guns" as they are sometimes described) and proceeded to drive off the Indians sniping from the far bank.

The expedition continued up the Yellowstone as far as Pompeys Pillar, where Sioux warriors fired on some troopers while they were swimming in the river, before doubling back along the Musselshell River to Stanley's Stockade. From there, the 7th Cavalry rode on to Fort Lincoln to universal acclaim. Custer, now commander of the Fort and Head of the Middle District of the Department of Dakota, kept six of his troops at Fort Lincoln, sent another four under Maj. Joseph Tilford south to Fort Rice and the remaining two, under Maj. Reno, north to Fort Totten.

In Custer's absence, wooden-frame buildings had sprung up at Fort Lincoln enabling it to accommodate the cavalry companies as well as three companies of infantry at the older post on the bluff a short distance to the north. One of the new, two-story structures was designated as the commanding officer's quarters and, after spending a month in Monroe, Autie brought Libbie back to her new home that he had secretly and comfortably furnished for her. She was delighted with her new quarters. The Custers and their coterie of friends soon became the center of an active social life during the first part of the winter of 1873-74, but on February 6, 1874 a chimney fire destroyed their new home. Autie managed to save his uniforms, but nearly everything else was lost. While the Custers took up temporary quarters, the post's carpenters put up a new two-story residence, even grander than the one they lost, with a bay window for Libbie and a library/den for Autie. One can assume that the weekly "hops," monthly "balls," and other social events continued without interruption.

Finding Custer Along the Missouri and Yellowstone Rivers

Today, a road sign on Highway 83, just north of Mound City, S.D., commemorates the march of the 7th Cavalry from Yankton to Fort Rice, as well as Gen. Alfred Sully's campaign against the Sioux in 1864, during which he established Fort Rice as his advanced base.

Fort Rice no longer exists, although the fort was named a state historical site early in the last century. Today, the Fort is remembered with some interpretive markers and a cannon to ward off the hordes of prairie dogs burrowed nearby. You can reach the site by driving a mile south on Highway 1806 from the town of Fort Rice.

Fort Abraham Lincoln is another story altogether, remaining a viable destination for tourists because many of the Fort's buildings have been rebuilt including barracks, the post granary and the quarters occupied by the Custers. It is possible to take a tour, conducted by a period-costumed guide, through the Custer House, which is decorated in the 1875 style. Armstrong's field desk is on display in what would have been his library/den. It is also possible to visit the site of an ancient Mandan Indian village and an interpretive center that puts the history of the Mandan village and the Fort in perspective.

Fort Abraham Lincoln State Park can be reached from Bismarck by driving across the Missouri River on I-94, exiting the Interstate at Mandan, and then taking Highway 1806 south for approximately nine miles. The Park has full camping facilities; the Fort itself has two cabins and two tipis for rent. Fort Lincoln is open daily from 9 a.m. to 5 p.m. Phone: (701) 667-6340. Various admission and use fees are charged.

While in Bismarck, you might want to visit St. Mary's Cemetery where Grant Marsh, the intrepid skipper of the steamboat *Far West* during the 1876 campaign, is buried. It is located at the corner of East Avenue D and 23rd Street.

Of course, Pompeys Pillar (named after Sacagawea's infant son, "Pomp," in 1806) still stands sentinel along the Yellowstone. It is now a National Historic Monument with all the amenities and can be reached by driving about 25 miles east of Billings on I-94. Leave the Interstate at the Highway 312 exit and follow the signs north to the Interpretive Center. If you climb the Pillar, you can see William Clark's signature carved in the rock with the date 1806 (the only on-site evidence of the Corps of Discovery's passing, although the Corps' campsites on the Missouri River are well marked, if only accessible by boat) and experience a somewhat tree-obstructed view of the river where the men of the 7th Cavalry were bathing when the Sioux opened fire on them. The Interpretive Center is closed from the end of September to early May, but the rest of the year the Pillar itself is still accessible by foot from the parking lot during daylight hours. Phone: (406) 875-2400.

The site of Custer's fight with the Sioux on August 4 (now often referred to as the Battle of Honsinger's Bluff) is unmarked, but if you cross the Yellowstone River at Miles City, Mont. on the Highway 59 bridge, and then drive up the northern bench to the airport, you will be near the site of the skirmish. Miles City is 144 miles east of Billings off I-94.

There is another location along the Missouri River that you might want to visit — the graves of scout William Brockmeyer, who was killed in a skirmish on August 2, 1876, and Pvt. William George, who was seriously wounded at the Little Bighorn and died on board the *Far West* as it raced downriver in an effort to get the 7th Cavalry wounded medical assistance at Bismarck. The graves are at the site of the Powder River Depot, the supply depot established by Gen. Terry at the confluence of the Powder and Yellowstone Rivers. The location is about halfway between Miles City and Glendive, Mont. To reach it, leave I-94 at Exit 169, just west from the Powder River crossing, drive west to old Highway 10; turn right (northeast) until you cross the old Powder River bridge. Then, turn left off Highway 10 just beyond the bridge, double back for a short distance before passing under the east abutment of the railroad bridge. Keep driving north out of the Powder River valley until you are on the bench above the river. The unimproved road splits off to the right in another quarter of a mile; follow the right-hand split north for about a half-mile to the remote gravesite.

Only attempt this side trip if you have a vehicle and tires up to the task, the roads are dry and as the weather permits.

The site is labeled on the Google Earth projection as "Scouts grave 1876." Using Google Earth will help you visualize the route.

THE BLACK HILLS EXCURSION 1874

Custer and the U.S. Army were caught up in the dynamics of western expansion in ways that probably seem excessive to Americans today. Not only had Gen. Sherman put the Army at the service of various railroad corporations, most recently the Northern Pacific, but he viewed rail construction as a positive way of bringing American civilization to the West and playing a role in ending the problems caused by a hostile Native American population. In the summer of 1874, Sherman and Sheridan were responsible for again unleashing another potent force in the epic conquest of the American West — the lure of gold.

Despite the solemn paragraphs in the 1868 Treaty of Fort Laramie giving the Sioux possession of the Black Hills in the Dakota Territory, persistent rumors of gold "in them thar hills" meant that white men, bedazzled by the lure of quick wealth, would soon demand access. That moment arrived in 1874 when Sheridan authorized an expedition, similar to the Yellowstone

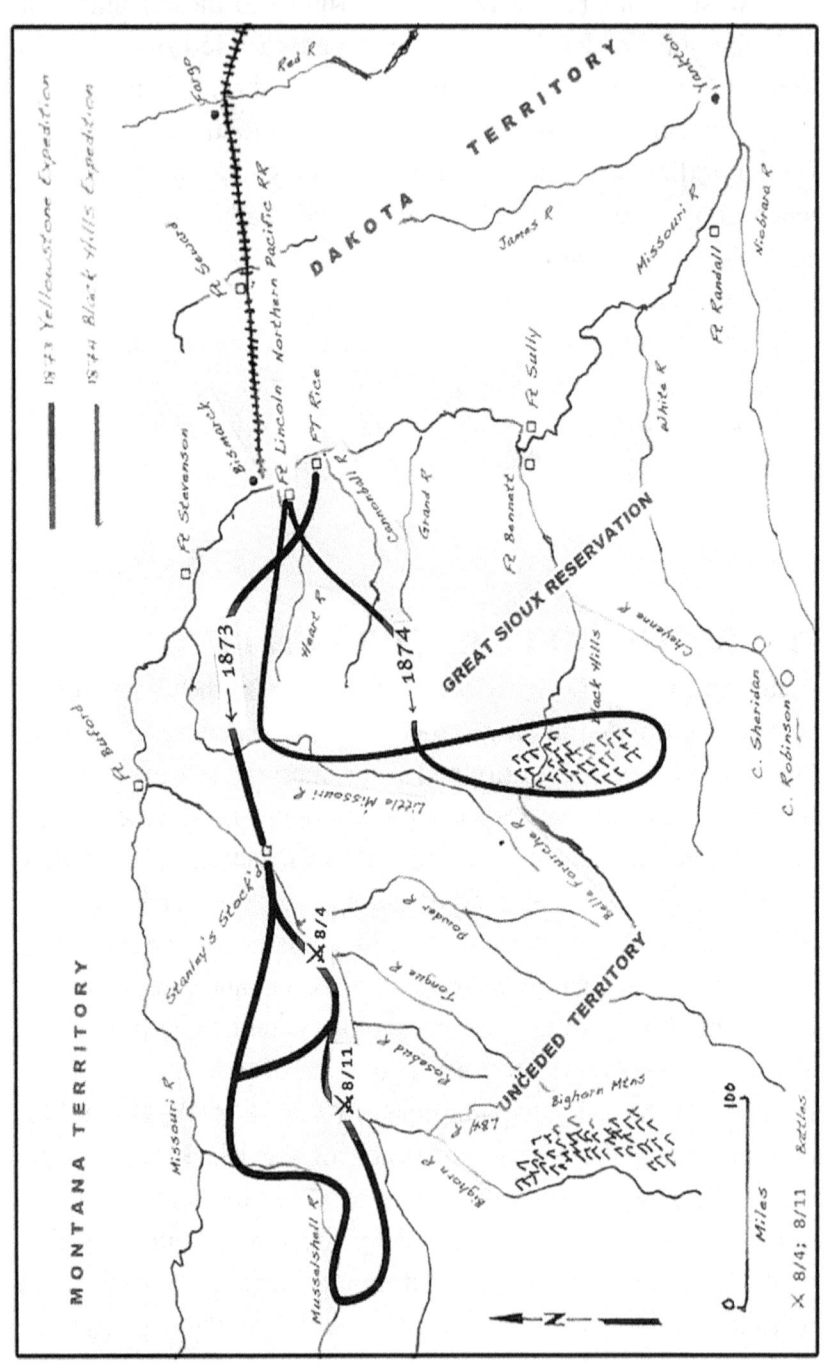

exploration of the previous summer, to reconnoiter the Black Hills with the hidden aim of settling the truth of the gold rumors and stated aim of determining the best location of a new fort in the mountains, which the Sioux considered sacred. The original intent was for Gen. Crook to lead the expedition from Fort Laramie, but Indian raids in Nebraska forced a change of plans. Again, Custer and the 7th Cavalry would provide an escort for the various scientists and miners who would carry out the expedition's purposes, stated and unstated.

The 7th Cavalry, minus the two troops on boundary survey duty, rode out of Fort Lincoln on July 2, 1874, to the strains of "The Girl I Left Behind Me," played by the regimental band mounted on their white horses. With the cavalry, the expedition numbered 951 individuals, including 75 scouts, two infantry companies guarding the hundred-plus wagons, an artillery battery, a pair of prospectors, engineers, geologists and the ubiquitous newspaper reporters. This formidable aggregation skirted the western side of the Hills, rounded their southern edge and returned to Fort Lincoln by traveling along their east side, arriving there on August 30, now to the strains of "Gary Owen." During those two months, they had encountered only Chief One Stab's small band of Sioux that Custer was barely able to save from being massacred by his Ree scouts. Armstrong scouted, hunted, and collected animals, dead and alive, along with mineral specimens to his heart's content. The entire expedition also found the Black Hills to be a delightful place in the summer with abundant game and clear streams teeming with trout.

But what about the gold? Prospectors William McKay and Horatio Nelson Ross worked the streams assiduously, finally turning up some sign on July 30 in French Creek. Many of the troopers reacted enthusiastically, one group forming a mining company and staking out claims, while others just spent their leisure time panning the gravel in the stream. There were some skeptics, among them Lt. Col. Fred Grant, the President's son, and Newton W. Winchell, the expedition's chief geologist. Their opinions counted for little since Custer had dispatched scout "Lonesome" Charley Reynolds to Fort Laramie with news of the strike, much exaggerated in the stories filed by the reporters accompanying the expedition. Gold fever struck the western frontier again, supported by another government survey in 1875 (one that Custer did not accompany). By the end of that year, there were an estimated 15,000 men seeking their fortunes in the Sioux's sacred Black Hills. Washington made another half-hearted effort to purchase the Hills from the Sioux, which only infuriated them more. Custer's route became known as the "Thieves' Road" and talk of armed resistance spread among the Lakota.

But what about the site for a new fort? Nothing about it was mentioned in Custer's official reports, but eventually, in 1878, two years after the battle of the Little Bighorn, the Army constructed Camp Sturgis on the plains near Bear Butte, Dakota Territory. The fort was appropriately named after Lt. "Jack" Sturgis, son of the regimental commander and himself commander of Company E, the "Gray Horse Troop," which the Lakota destroyed at the Little Bighorn. Soon a permanent post was built nearer to the foothills and south of Bear Butte Creek. First named Camp Ruhlen after the officer in charge of its construction, the Army renamed the new post Fort Meade in honor of the former commander of the Army of the Potomac, Gen. George G. Meade. (Note: The Fort is still used by the South Dakota National Guard as a training site, houses a National Guard Officer's Candidate School, and is the site of a museum.)

Finding Custer in the Black Hills
The Black Hills Expedition camped at Hiddenwood Cliff, near Haynes, ND on July 8, 1874. Informative signs mark the campsite today. Haynes is located off Highway 12 in the far southwest corner of the state.

On July 22 the Expedition reached the foot of Inyan Kara, a geologically unusual mountain in the northern Black Hills some 1,600 feet in elevation. The next day, Armstrong, Maj. George A. Forsyth, Capt. William Ludlow and a few other intrepid souls climbed to the top. Armstrong left his mark on the mountain by scratching "74 G Custer" on a rock face.

It is possible to climb the mountain today to view Custer's graffiti with prior permission from the U.S. Forest Service. Trail permits and visitor information can be obtained at the Pactola Visitor Center west of Rapid City on Highway 385, which is open every day from Memorial Day through Labor Day weekend from 9 a.m. to 5 p.m. Phone: (605) 343-8755 and from the Black Hills Visitor Center, located off I-90 at Exit 61. Inyan Kara is located in the Bearlodge Ranger District. The District office is in Sundance, Wyo. and is open Monday through Friday from 8 a.m. to 4:30 p.m. Phone: (307) 283-3727.

The 7th Cavalry also buried two of its deceased troopers, John Cunningham (chronic diarrhea) and George Turner (shot during a quarrel), near their camp at the foot of the mountain.

Inyan Kara, a state historical marker and a small, enclosed graveyard, which may not actually contain the bodies of the troopers, can be reached from I-90 by exiting at Exit 187 and driving about 15 miles south on Highway 585.

On the last day of that July, Armstrong, Ludlow and others climbed Harney Peak (Hinhan Kaga to the Sioux), the highest mountain in the Black Hills at 7,242 feet and considered the highest peak in the United States east of the Rockies. Harney Peak stands 3.7 miles southwest of Mount Rushmore. At this date, the mountain remains Harney Peak, despite concerted efforts to change the name to Hinhan Kaga.

The easiest hiking route (7 miles) to the summit begins at Sylvan Lake in Custer State Park. Check with the Forest Service about permits before attempting the climb.

Other Interesting Destinations in the Black Hills

When you have exhausted Custeriana in the Black Hills, turn your attention to the many other interesting places to visit. Since there are ample guides to the Hills, we will simply list some of the more prominent destinations:

Devil's Tower

Sturgis, during the late summer motorcycle rally

Mount Rushmore

Crazy Horse Memorial

Bridal Veil Falls near Spearfish

Bear Mountain

Slim Butte Battlefield

Deadwood

Rapid City

Fort Meade

The Custers spent only part of the winter of 1874-75 at Fort Lincoln and Libbie found the routine much the same as in the previous year. In the fall, they lived for six weeks in Monroe, visiting friends and family. In late December, they again caught the train east; Armstrong first meeting with Sheridan at his headquarters in Chicago before traveling to New York City in an unsuccessful effort to raise capital for a Colorado mining venture. The Custers did not return to Fort Lincoln until June 1875.

Sheridan had assigned the 1875 Black Hills expedition to George Crook's command based at Fort Laramie, so the 7th Cavalry spent a relatively uneventful summer policing the northern plains, although the Sioux and Cheyenne became increasingly angry at another blatant incursion into their heartland that they considered a gross violation of the Fort Laramie Treaty. While the official policy of the United States was to uphold the provisions of the treaty prohibiting whites from settling or even entering or crossing the Great Sioux Reservation, it became the unofficial policy of both Custer and Crook to ignore any violations. In an effort to convince the tribes to sell the Black Hills, the Grant Administration arranged for Chiefs Red Cloud and Spotted Tail to visit Washington in May, but the two old warriors were unmoved. The Secretary of the Interior also appointed a commission, the Allison Commission, to deal with the tribes on their own ground. The meeting of the Commissioners with some 5,000 Indians at the Red Cloud Agency in western Nebraska in September came to naught as the younger tribesmen threatened the older chiefs with violence if they agreed to part with the Black Hills. The Commissioners were furious at this rebuff, so in their report they advised that the U.S. government offer a fair price for the Hills and, if rejected, cut off all rations and subsidies. However, they doubted that the Sioux would budge until they were made to feel the military might of the United States.

An exasperated Grant administration now moved quickly, if surreptitiously, to solve its Indian problem on the northern plains. Earlier, in June, Sheridan sent a party of officers up the Yellowstone by steamboat to reconnoiter sites for two new forts. Now, in the aftermath of the Allison Commission fiasco, President Grant met with Gens. Sheridan and Crook, Secretary of

War William W. Belknap, Secretary of the Interior Zachariah Chandler and the Commissioner of Indian Affairs in the White House on November 3, 1875. Two momentous decisions emerged from this meeting: (1) the Army, despite the provisions in the Fort Laramie Treaty, would no longer enforce the ban on non-Indians in the Black Hills, although the ban itself would remain in effect; and (2) the "year-around-roamers," mainly Hunkpapa Sioux under the charismatic Sitting Bull, would be ordered to abandon their nomadic life for residency on a reservation. Less than a week later, the Indian Inspector, Erwin C. Watkins issued a report based on his recent inspection of Missouri River agencies that called for military action to "whip them (the year-around-roamers) into subjection." The decision was quickly made that if the "roamers" did not report to their reservations by the end of January 1876, preparations would begin for a late winter military campaign to force compliance. When the message was delivered to their winter camps in January, the "roamers" naturally ignored the government's demands (there was no way they could move that distance in mid-winter), and so the stage was set for the Sioux War of 1876, a contrived and immoral conflict if ever there was one.

POLITICS: 1875-76

Custer had meanwhile made the mistake of embroiling himself in Washington politics. He and Libbie spent their annual winter leave in New York City, where Autie worked on his memoir of the Kansas years, published as "My Life on the Plains," in which he wrote of his ambivalent feelings toward the Indians. "If I were an Indian," he mused, "I often think that I would greatly prefer to cast my lot among those of my people who adhered to the free open plains, rather than submit to the confined limits of a reservation ... ." Many other Army officers who served in the Indian Wars expressed similar feelings, even guilt for their participation in warfare that often meant attacking villages of women and children as well as the warriors who defended them.

But, it was politics not humanitarianism that almost undid Armstrong. A long time Democrat, he allowed himself to be used by Congressional Democrats and their newspaper-owner allies in their maneuvering to bring down the Secretary of the Interior, Columbus Delano, over the selling of sutler concessions at western Army posts by Orvil Grant, the president's corrupt younger brother. Apparently, the Secretary of War, William W. Belknap, was guilty of taking kickbacks as well; he resigned in March 1876 after the House voted to impeach him. Sutlers, who had purchased their commissions at a hefty price, were not reluctant to recoup their investments by overcharging soldiers for their wares. Some of Custer's biographers even think that he toyed with becoming involved in a similar scheme with the notorious entrepreneur, Ben Holladay. After Armstrong's death, Frederick Benteen accused him of having sold sutler appointments for both the Yellowstone and Black Hills Expeditions. But, Benteen was so consumed with hatred for Custer that it is impossible to take any of his claims at face value. Armstrong was also blind to the nepotism involved in rewarding his relatives throughout his career; we mustn't forget, it was "The Gilded Age," when such favoritism was widely practiced and usually accepted.

In any event, Custer agreed to testify before two congressional committees concerning the corruption in the granting of sutler concessions, and his testimony put him in serious disfavor with his commander-in-chief, President Grant, because it implicated Orvil Grant. It is doubtful if the congressional Democrats who lunched with Custer were as interested in reforming the sutler system as they were in embarrassing the administration and Armstrong became their tool. Besides, his testimony was largely hearsay. On one occasion, when he appeared at the White House to pay a courtesy visit before returning to his post, Grant let him cool his heels in his waiting room for four hours before having an orderly dismiss him. Believing that he was done with Washington politics, Custer left the capital, and, after a brief stop in Monroe, was waiting in Chicago to catch the Northern Pacific back to Fort Lincoln, when he was handed a telegram from Sherman telling him to await further orders and to allow the Dakota column to march without him. Sherman permitted Custer to travel to St. Paul where he met with Gen. Terry to draft a telegram pleading with Grant to reconsider. The President relented, but stipulated that Custer was to command the 7th Cavalry only, giving Terry command of the Dakota column. Not until May 10th did Terry and Custer board the train for Bismarck, much too late for any winter campaign.

CENTENNIAL CAMPAIGN, 1876

The plan for the "Centennial Campaign" against the Sioux and their Cheyenne allies was much like that employed in other campaigns against the Plains Tribes — utilize converging columns to harass Indian bands, and thus convince them to give up their nomadic ways for a settled life on designated reservations. The plan for the spring of 1876 called for three Army columns to converge on the unceded Indian Territory. Gen. George Crook would move north from Fort Fetterman along the old Bozeman Trail route, while Col. John Gibbon would march from Fort Ellis on the Madison River to a blocking position along the north bank of the Yellowstone to prevent the "roamers" from escaping to the north. The Terry-Custer column, comprised of the 7th Cavalry and assorted supporting troops, including soldiers from the 20th Infantry along to man three Gatling Guns, was the principal strike force that was ordered to move west from Fort Abraham Lincoln to a rendezvous with the other columns in the heart of the unceded territory. Because of the last spring jump off date, logistical support and communications would rely on wagon and pack trains and the occasional telegraphic link. (As it turned out, the delays meant that the rivers were open to navigation, thus the steamboats *Far West* and *Josephine*, under contract to the Army, would play a vital role in supporting the campaign.)

Gen. Crook was first off the mark, marching out of Fort Fetterman on the 1st of March right into the face of a raging blizzard. Crook's force numbered just under 700 men irrespective of civilian scouts, packers, drovers and teamsters. The wagons and pack mules (in his earlier campaigns, Crook had pioneered the use of pack mules in Indian warfare) carried two weeks' worth of provisions. Two weeks later, after having allowed hostile Indians to run off his cattle herd, his scouts located an Indian camp on the upper reaches of the Powder River. For some undisclosed reason, Crook, who rarely revealed his plans or discussed them with subordinates, allowed Col. Joseph J. Reynolds, a 54-year-old Civil War veteran and titular commander of the column, to attack the camp on the bitterly cold morning of March 17. Reynolds, who was probably too old to lead any campaign, much less a late winter campaign, botched the effort, precipitously retreating in the face of an Indian counterattack. Crook, maintaining the fiction that he was only along an observer, had remained back with the infantry and pack train, now abandoned his march north to retreat south to Fort Fetterman where he had Reynolds court-martialed; found guilty, Reynolds retired from the Army in 1877. The attack at the Powder River was not an auspicious beginning for the campaign, nor did reflect well on Crook's command abilities. His sterling reputation as an Indian fighter was based on his earlier campaigns against the Paiutes in Oregon and the Apaches in Arizona, but he botched his three engagements with the Sioux and Cheyenne during 1876-77.

Next to march was Col. John Gibbon, commander of the 7th Infantry. With his foot soldiers and a battalion of the 2nd Cavalry, some 500 men in total, he left Fort Ellis near Bozeman, Montana Territory, in nasty weather on April 3. Gibbon then headed down the Yellowstone River to cut off any Indian bands that might try to flee north in an effort to reach the Canadian border. Gibbon's Crow scouts actually located a large Indian camp in the Rosebud valley on May 27, but he failed to act on this intelligence or, inexplicably, to inform Gen. Terry of this discovery. By the middle of June, Gibbon's isolated column was camped on the north bank of the Yellowstone across from the mouth of Rosebud Creek.

The Terry-Custer column was the last to take the field for reasons that have been dealt with above. As it started west from Fort Lincoln on the foggy, raw morning of May 17, the 7th Cavalry Regiment was an impressive sight. The Regiment was now at full troop strength with four troops having been recalled from Reconstruction duty, however each of the individual troops was badly understrength. The column also included three companies of infantry, Indian scouts, the Gatling gun battery, numerous wagons and a beef herd. Armstrong's family retinue included his younger brothers, Tom, Company C commander, and Boston, a forage master, his brother-in-law, Capt. Frederick Calhoun, who commanded Company L, and his nephew, herder Armstrong "Autie" Reed. All would perish at the Little Bighorn. The column stretched for two-miles as it swung west to the inevitable strains of "The Girl I Left Behind Me." Libbie and "Sister Margaret" (Maggie Calhoun) rode with it for the first day. As the mist lifted, Libbie remembered a "scene of wonder and beauty," a mirage appearing over "about half the line of cavalry, and thenceforth for a little distance it marched, equally plain to the sight on the earth and in the sky." In the morning, they watched the column ford the Heart River before sadly returning to Fort Lincoln. Their husbands, of course, would both fall in the coming battle.

There was some thought that the Dakota Column might meet the Sioux as soon as the Little Missouri River. However, if the staff had done its intelligence work properly, it would have learned from the scouts that the "year-around-wanderers" were likely to be 150 miles farther to the west on the Tongue or Rosebud or Bighorn Rivers, soon to be joined by bands from the reservations, the "summer wanderers," who planned to spend the summer months hunting with their more recalcitrant kinsmen. Progress of the Dakota column was slow, but steady. Streams often had to be crossed on pontoon bridges. On reaching the Little Missouri, Custer scouted down to its mouth without finding any sign of the year-around-wanderers. On June 7, the column reached the Powder River. From there, Terry and Custer rode to its junction with the Yellowstone where they met Gibbon who had come down river on the *Far West*.

None of the commanders had any hard intelligence on the whereabouts of Sitting Bull and his allies. Their last location, determined by Lt. James H. Bradley, head of Gibbon's Crow scouts, was that about 400 lodges were on Rosebud Creek, but that information was a month old. To determine the current location of the camps, Terry ordered the right wing of the 7th Cavalry, under Marcus Reno, (six troops, scouts, and a Gatling gun) on a "reconnaissance" up the Powder River, across the divide to the Tongue, and then down that river to its junction with the Yellowstone. Terry's orders were very specific: Reno was to provision himself for 12 days and follow the specific route outlined in his orders. The unanswered question in those orders was what should Reno do if he discovered the Indian camp, wait for reinforcement or engage? The great flaw in this "reconnaissance plan" in Custer's view, other than he was not commanding it, was that the Sioux might detect Reno's presence and scatter before real force could be brought against them. Terry disagreed.

Reno's column marched on June 10. Five days later, he was moving down the Tongue when he came upon a large, abandoned Indian camp that his chief scout, Mitch Boyer, estimated at 400 lodges. At this point, Reno chose to disregard his orders by moving west to Rosebud Creek, which he scouted upstream for a short distance before turning downstream to rendezvous on the Yellowstone with Terry and Custer. Both his superiors were furious that he had disobeyed his orders by moving to the Rosebud, but actually Reno had made a solid contribution toward locating the hostile camp. By eliminating the upper Rosebud from consideration and determining that the camp had moved west, Reno's reconnaissance helped Terry formulate a new, more flexible plan that would send Custer with both wings of the 7th Cavalry up the shallow creek as a highly mobile strike force. Leaving a few infantry companies with untrained and unhorsed recruits behind to guard the supply depot, Terry could then move his and Gibbon's remaining companies to the mouth of the Bighorn River to block any Indians trying to escape north by crossing the Yellowstone, headed for the Canadian border. Terry drafted written orders for Custer on June 21 that were quite different in the latitude they granted him than the ones he had given to Reno 12 days before. In edited form, his orders read, "… the Department Commander places too much confidence in your zeal, energy and ability to wish to impose on you precise orders which might hamper your action when nearly in contact with the enemy. He will, however, indicate to you his own views of what your action should be, and he desires that you should conform to them unless *you* (italics added) shall see sufficient reason for departing from them." As John S. Gray wrote in his 1976 monograph, "Centennial Campaign," that after reading these orders, "One may quarrel with Custer's judgment, but not his authority to judge. Custer's obedience is therefore neither debatable, nor relevant." Some writers have quibbled over the words "nearly in contact," but they have missed the tenor of Terry's orders.

The 7th Cavalry, badly understrength at 597 officers and men, began its fateful movement up the Rosebud in the early afternoon of June 22. There were no bugles blaring or bands playing or wives weeping as the Regiment passed in review. Urged by a white scout, the Rees sang their death songs as if they knew their fate. Terry, Gibbon, Custer and the troopers they reviewed also thought they knew what was to come in the days ahead. They had no idea. They expected to track down and engage Sitting Bull's camp of Sioux and Cheyenne totaling about 400 lodges housing maybe 800 warriors. Despite warnings from their Ree and Crow scouts, they were blind to the number of "summer wanderers" who were leaving their reservation to join Sitting Bull. The number of warriors they would eventually face was easily double the number anticipated. They would discount their scouts' alarm at discovering a solitary tipi where the Sioux had held their sacred sun-dance ceremony in preparation for battle. They failed completely to understand the desperation these people felt knowing the United States and its Army was moving against them with the object of removing them from their sacred lands and snuffing out their ancestral way of life. Custer and the left wing of the 7th Cavalry would pay the ultimate price for their obtuseness. They had committed the cardinal mistake in warfare — they underestimated their enemy.

And, what was Gen. Crook engaged in during this critical period? The answer would seem to be tripping over his own bootlaces. After reinforcing his column to a total of over 1,300 men, he struck north again on a halcyon May 29 for Fort Reno, where he hoped to find a contingent of Crow and Shoshone scouts. The good marching weather ended abruptly when the column was hit by an unexpected spring snowstorm three days later. More serious was the fact that no Indian scouts had yet reported for duty, so Crook made camp at Ft. Reno before sending his three white scouts to the Crow Agency to recruit young warriors. Meanwhile, Crook took it upon himself to guide the column north, but just past Fetterman Hill he lost his way and then decided to go to ground until help arrived. In the evening of June 9, Crook's camp was hit by a Sioux raiding party that accomplished nothing for its trouble. Crook responded by backtracking so as to pick up the correct trail and then going to ground again. Finally, on June 14, much to Crook's relief, the first Crow scouts showed up and, after lengthy negotiations, many signed on for the campaign. Soon, the Shoshone contingent reported in as well, giving Crook the courage to move north once again. At this point, he left his wagons and pack train behind, provisioning his men with four days' rations as they struck north down the Rosebud without a clue as to the true location of Sitting Bull's camp. The infantrymen rode the unhappy, thus ornery, pack mules.

On the 17th, Crook's scouts reported finding signs of hostile Indians prompting Crook to halt his column in a narrow valley surrounded by bluffs and allow his men to unsaddle and rest along both sides of Rosebud Creek. After about an hour, the Sioux struck, fought off at first only by the Crow and Shoshone scouts. Crook eventually disengaged half of his men under the command of Capt. Anson Mills to attack the Indian camp that he erroneously estimated to be only five or six miles away. When the narrowing canyon blocked the movement of this detachment, Crook ordered it back into the fight where it was then able to outflank and drive off the attacking warriors. The Battle of the Rosebud thus ended in a draw. Crook suffered about 70 casualties. (His Indian scouts lifted 13 scalps.) Low on ammunition and with dwindling rations, he retreated back to his base camp on Goose Creek, claiming a victory in his dispatch to Gen. Sheridan on June 19. Three days later, when Custer began his movement up the Rosebud, Crook had long since departed the scene.

TO THE LITTLE BIGHORN, JUNE 22-25, 1876

Because of John S. Gray's time/motion studies of both the campaign and the Battle of the Little Bighorn, we now have a reasonably accurate idea of the movement of the 7th Cavalry from the time it left the Yellowstone River on June 22 until its survivors were found by the Terry-Gibbon column on June 28. In a greatly abbreviated form, we will attempt to follow Gray's sequence of events as he developed them in "Custer's Last Campaign" (1991). The times and distances given are, of course, approximate.

The first day's march was a short 12 miles up the left bank of the Rosebud. The column got underway by 5 a.m. the next morning and passed the first abandoned Sioux campsite at 7:40, a second at 10:20 and a third about three hours later. The regiment made camp at 4:30 p.m. after traveling 33 miles in 11 hours at an average pace of 3 miles per hour. Scouts had not yet sighted any hostile Indians. Custer held an officers call that evening during which he encouraged his officers to do their duty in the coming days; he also gave them an estimate of the strength of Sitting Bull's camp derived from information he had obtained from the Indian Office. He estimated the year-around-roamers to number about 3,000 individuals, giving them a fighting strength of something like 850 to 1,000 warriors, a number he thought the 7th Cavalry could easily handle.

The day began much the same on the 24th. Troopers were in the saddle at 5 a.m., as was the cavalry's routine. An hour and a half later the column halted a mile above another deserted campsite, this being the one where Sitting Bull interpreted his vision during the sun-dance as prophesying victory over the white soldiers, and then moved into the camp to examine it and the soldiers' scalps they found in the sun-dance lodge. Since the afternoon of the previous day, Custer had his Ree and Crow scouts out in force probing ahead for the mobile enemy camp. They now reported that the hostile camp had moved west across the Wolf Mountain divide to the Little Bighorn at the Busby bend of the Rosebud, but did not know where it was presently located. The regiment set up camp on the Rosebud near the mouth of Davis Creek at about 7:45 p.m. that evening. They were 72 miles from their starting point on the Yellowstone.

Following Custer to The Little Bighorn
The Custer Auto Tour

The 7th Cavalry followed the route through the Dakota Territory taken earlier by Gens. Sully and Stanley and Maj. Whistler, that essentially followed the Heart River west until it petered out in the Badlands just before it reached the Little Missouri River near the border of the Montana Territory. Today, no major roads follow that route, but it is possible to drive part of the Terry/Custer column's trail where it crossed the Little Missouri, thanks to the USFS having established and marked the "Custer Auto Tour" in 2005. To do that will entail a 100-mile detour south of I-94 through the Little Missouri National Grassland that will take approximately a day to drive. The Auto Tour has seven stops:

>1) The Easy Hill Overlook where Armstrong sought to identify landmarks from his traverse with the Stanley Expedition of 1873.
>2) The Easy Hill Camp Site where the column camped overnight.
>3) Initial Rock. On May 28, two troopers in the rear guard, Frank Neely and William C. Williams, carved their names in a sandstone rock. Their names,

covered today with glass, are still visible. Both men, in Reno's command, survived the coming battle.
4) The column's campsite for May 29 and 30 has now morphed into the Bully Pulpit Golf Course. There is a plaque on the grounds commemorating that stop.
5) The Snow Camp where the column was snowed in for two nights on May 31 and June 1.
6) Sully's Waterhole. Gen. Sully's column stopped here in 1865 to water horses and replenish canteens.
7) The Battle of the Badlands site is near Square Butte where on August 8-9, 1865 Sully's troops fought a running battle with the Sioux.

Your detour should begin with a stop at the Painted Canyon Visitor Center and Rest Area, which is located just north of I-94 at Exit 32. This exit is 8.38 miles east of the town of Medora, N.D. (Exit 24). Forest Service personnel at the Center can provide you with maps and current information concerning the auto tour. The Visitor Center is open seasonally from June to October. From June 1 to mid-August its hours are 8:00 a.m. to 6:00 p.m. daily; from mid-August to mid-October hours are 9:30 a.m. to 4:30 p.m. daily.

We have decided to limit our driving instructions to those sites actually visited by Custer and the 7th Cavalry in 1876, omitting the Sully places of interest. Be forewarned that today the roads wind through the Grasslands primarily to service the numerous well sites in the Bakken oil field.

To begin the tour at the Visitor Center, drive under the Interstate on Forest Road (FR) 739A to FR 739; continue south on FRs 722 and 762 to Easy Hill and the Easy Hill campsite. Backtrack to the west on FR 762 and FR 740 to the Initial Rock campsite. From there, drive northwest on FR 740 and FR 742 to the campsite at the Bully Pulpit Golf Course. From the golf course, it's a 3-mile drive north on FR 762 and FH 3 to Medora, which is an interesting town for a lunch stop or an overnight stay. The town has four rated hotels/motels, the Rough Riders Hotel being a traveler's favorite, along with its Theodore's Restaurant.

To actually visit the site of the Snow Camp (May 31 and June 1) requires a 2-mile hike south from Old Highway 10 (OH 10), but a roadside marker points out the location of the campsite. To find the marker from Medora, rejoin the Interstate traveling west. Take the next Exit 23, and then drive south on the West River Road until it intersects with OH 10. Follow OH 10 to the marker. From there you can continue on OH 10 to the town of Beach, where there is another commemorative marker to the passing of Custer and the 7th Cavalry.

At Beach, rejoin I-94 at Exit 1 and drive west toward Glendive where it meets the Yellowstone River, and then turns southwest toward Miles City, Mont.

The Route from the Yellowstone to the Little Bighorn:
Probably the best way to trace the 7th Cavalry's route from the Yellowstone River to the Little Bighorn Battlefield is to leave I-94 at Exit 103 about 33 miles west of Miles City.

Before beginning that excursion, you can drive to a marker commemorating the fateful June 22 meeting aboard the steamboat *Far West* when Terry wrote the orders that unleashed Custer. To do so, leave the Interstate to the north before swinging east on the frontage road (OH 10). In a mile you will reach the junction with Highway 446. Turn left and cross the Yellowstone River. Just across the river, take the fishing access road back to the west and follow it to the marker. The fishing access point is directly opposite the mouth of the Rosebud where the *Far West* was moored.

The route that Custer followed up the Rosebud to the Wolf Mountain divide today is now Highway 447 and marked by signs found near the 7th Cavalry's campsites. To follow that route, recross the Yellowstone River, turn west to the I-94 exit, and then drive south on Highway 447 (the Rosebud Creek Road.)

In about seven miles, you will pass a marker for the presumed grave of trooper Nathan Short, who is thought, without valid supporting evidence, to be buried here. The marker for the 7th Cavalry's first campsite (June 22) is about four miles farther along Highway 447. Custer pushed his command hard the next day, covering some 33 miles. You will find a marker at the June 23 campsite as well. On the third day, the column rode 27 miles to the present site of Busby, Mont. where the 7th's final campsite is located. Nearby a stone memorial stands atop Chief Two Moons' grave. From Busby, you can drive 24 miles south to the site of Crook's fight on the Rosebud (Rosebud Battlefield State Park) or continue west on Highway 212 through the Wolf Mountains to the Little Bighorn Battlefield National Monument.

Custer now faced a critical decision. If he followed his orders to the letter, he would continue up the Rosebud for at least another day before moving west to the upper reaches of the Little Bighorn, where Terry had expected him to find the Sitting Bull's camp. That movement would allow Terry and Gibbon to reach their blocking position at the mouth of the Bighorn on June 26, still two days away. But, Custer now realized that the hostile camp was on the lower section of the Little Bighorn and to continue south now made little sense, as it would expose his column to detection. As one would expect, Custer chose the bolder course. Informed by his scouts that the valley of the Little Bighorn could be seen from a high point in the Wolf Mountains, he chose to send Lt. Charles A. Varnum with 13 scouts, including Mitch Boyer and "Lonesome" Charlie Reynolds, forward to an overlook, the "Crow's Nest," while the column followed them up Davis Creek in a rugged night march. The regiment would remain hidden on the 25th, and after another night march would attack the hostile camp at dawn on the 26th. Custer informed his officers of his intentions at a nighttime officer's call.

The main column set off at about 12:30 a.m. and halted at 3:15 a.m. for a break. The troopers slept until sunrise, then breakfasted and slept again. They were in the saddle at 8:45 a.m., rode for an hour and a half before halting again just before the divide. By then, Custer had himself ridden to the Crow's Nest to meet with Varnum's party, returning to the main column at 10:35 a.m. Various sightings of hostile Indians now convinced him that the column had been detected and that any delay now would allow the hostile village to scatter. He held another officer's call a little before 11:00 to announce his decision to attack at once and then divided the column into four battalions. He ordered his Crow scouts to concentrate on capturing the large pony herd grazing west of the village.

CUSTER HILL, JUNE 25, 1876

The 7th Cavalry crossed the divide to the headwaters of Reno Creek at noon on the 25th of June knowing now that there would be no repeat of the Washita surprise dawn-attack. The still largely invisible Indian village, spread out over several miles on the far side of the Little Bighorn, lay about 15 miles to the Northwest.

After a two-hour ride, five miles above the mouth of Reno Creek, the command passed a solitary tipi containing the body of a dead warrior. The time was 2:15 p.m. Reports that the column had been definitely sighted caused Custer to order Reno's battalion (Troops A, G and M, about 145 men) to advance at the trot, giving assurance that he would support him. By 3:03 p.m., Reno's troopers watered their horses while fording the Little

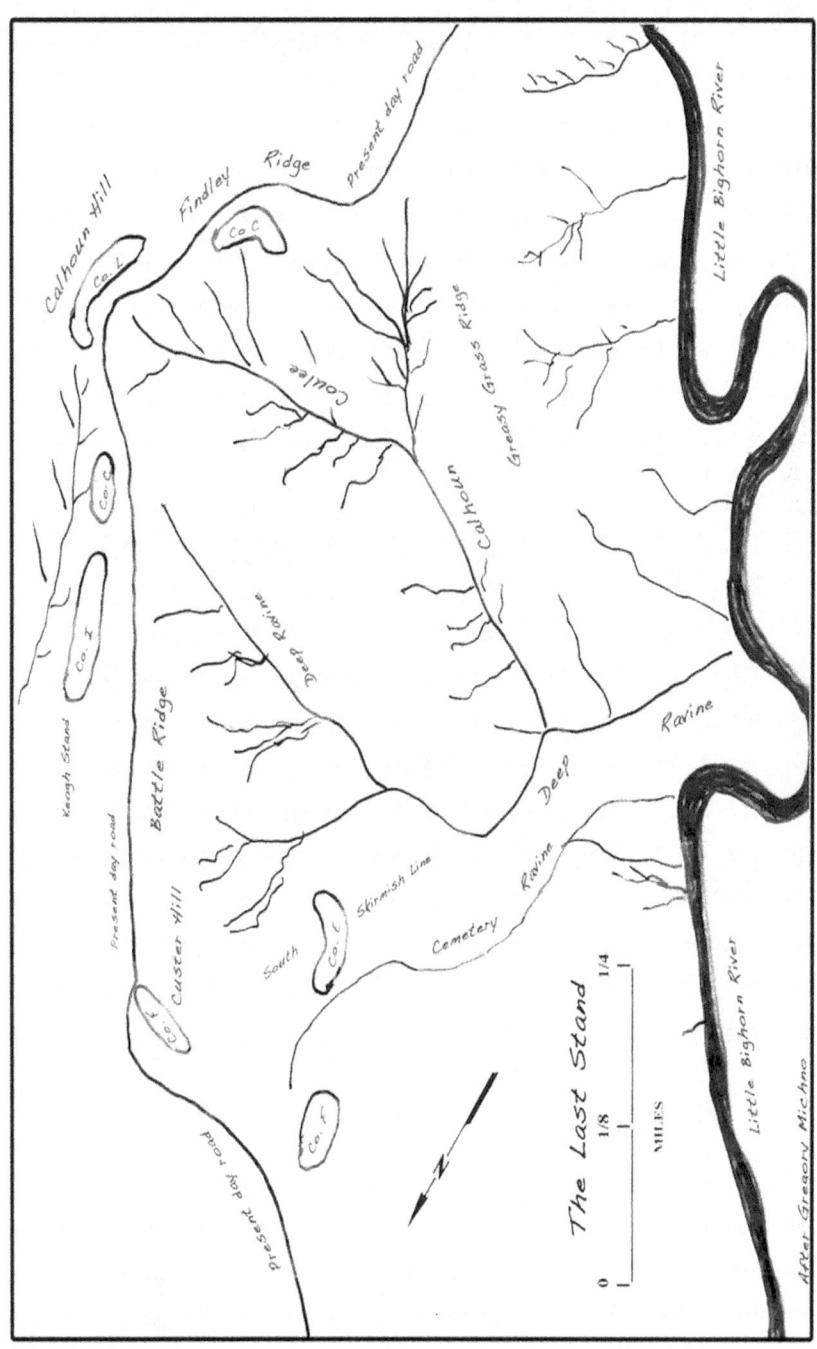

Last Stand Map (Stephen T. Powers)

Bighorn, deployed in a line on the west bank flats (two troops forward, one in reserve) and were now in position to begin their charge toward the south end of the Indian camp.

Before leaving the noon halt on the divide, Custer ordered Benteen's battalion (Troops D, H and K, about 125 men) on a scouting mission to the west to ensure that no Indians were slipping away upriver. Although ordered to complete his scout quickly and rejoin Custer as rapidly as possible, Benteen dawdled, not returning to the Reno-Custer trail until it was too late to reinforce either Reno or Custer in their desperate attacks. Nor did he report to Custer the vital information that his scouts had seen no sign of Indians fleeing south along the Little Bighorn valley. His command eventually reached Reno Hill at 4:20 p.m., where it reinforced Reno's already shattered battalion.

Custer's command (Capt. George W. Yates' battalion, Troops E and F and Capt. Miles W. Keogh's battalion, Troops C, I and L, about 206 men in all) rode down the right bank of Reno Creek trailing Reno by a few minutes. Before reaching the Little Bighorn and believing that the Indian camp was in full flight, Custer veered sharply to the right, leaving Reno's trail to climb the high bluffs east of the river. Custer, aggressive as usual and confident in his abilities as a combat commander, intended to envelope the camp in a pincer movement rather than simply trail behind Reno' charge. It was only when he reached a high point above the river, (later to become known as Reno Hill,) that he had a full view of the Indian camp and could appreciate its size. According to trumpeter John Martin, (né Giovanni Martini, one of the many immigrant members of the 7th Cavalry), when Custer saw the camp, he is reported to have waved his hat, shouting: "Courage, boys, we have got them. And soon as we get through, we will go back to our station." However, a few minutes later he sent back Sgt. Daniel Kanipe with orders for Benteen and the pack train "to come on quick." Kanipe delivered his message to Benteen at 3:42 and the pack train six minutes later. After

Custer returned from a brief side trip to a nearby high point (Weir Peak) to assess his situation, he had his adjutant Lt. William W. Cooke dispatch Martin with the urgent message: "Benteen. Come on. Big village. Be Quick. Bring pack. W.W. Cooke, PS bring pacs." It was now 3:34 p.m.

Reno began his charge on the Indian camp a few minutes after three o'clock. Very quickly a large group of mounted warriors appeared between his line and the first tipis, and then the fight began in earnest. Reno ordered his troopers to dismount and form an open skirmish line, a wise move given the 2,000 or so warriors his 145 men faced. His battalion held its ground for 15 or 20 minutes, before he ordered a remount and retreat into the cottonwoods along the river to his right. Shortly thereafter, Reno's face was splattered with the gore from a fatal head-wound suffered by his Ree scout, Bloody Knife, who was riding alongside him. Most likely unnerved, Reno shouted for his men to follow him and then he raced for the timber. At that moment, his battalion began to disintegrate. Unable to reform a defense in the trees bordering the Little Bighorn, his troopers remounted and forded the river in order to scramble to safety up the bluffs on the far bank, leaving a number of their comrades behind. The retreat now became a rout as mounted warriors rode among the fleeing troopers shooting them down as if they were a stampeding herd of buffalo. Thirty-one of the 35 troopers lost in this action were killed in their panicked flight across the river. Some of those left behind in the cottonwoods hid out until they were able to rejoin the other survivors the following day. Reno's demoralized cavalrymen, now grouped on a low knob that became known as Reno Hill, were saved only because of the large number of warriors who broke off their attack after word had reached them of Custer's flanking movement along the bluffs, and, later, by the timely arrival of Benteen's battalion trailed by the pack train.

As the day began, Boston, the youngest of the Custer brothers, had been tagging along with the pack train. As the mules passed the lone tipi at 2:45 p.m., Boston decided to ride ahead to join his brothers, which he did an hour later at the bottom of Cedar Coulee. He passed Benteen's battalion on his 6.5-mile ride, proving that Benteen was not pushing very hard to rejoin the main body. Boston ran into trooper Martin at the head of Cedar Coulee. Martin warned him of Indians ahead, but Boston indicated that he was going to continue on anyway, joining his brothers at 3:49 p.m. undoubtedly imparting the encouraging news that Benteen's battalion and the pack train could not be far behind.

Keogh-Crazy Horse Fight (Photo: Dave Taylor)

Not finding a ford to his liking at the bottom of Cedar Coulee, Custer pulled back to higher ground before turning back toward the river by moving down Medicine Tail Coulee. Here, scouts Mitch Boyer and Curley rejoined the column with word of

Reno's defeat and flight. He released his scouts at this point; Curley rode off to the east, while Mitch Boyer elected to stay with the command. Custer now must have realized that the tactical situation facing his battalion was precarious, for the Sioux and Cheyenne warriors, freed from the threat posed by Reno's attack, were able to concentrate on the 200-odd men under his immediate command. Now, he split his battalion into two wings, the one (Troops C, I and L) under the hard-drinking Irish Captain, Myles W. Keogh and the other (Troops F, the Band Box Troop and E, the Gray Horse Troop) went to his old friend, Capt. George Yates. The time was 4:04 p.m. In a little over an hour, the fight would be over and the battalion no more.

Historians of various degrees of talent and bias have tried since 1876 to unravel the events of that hour with widely differing degrees of success. In the opinion of the authors, some of the best contemporary efforts are those of Robert M. Utley, Jeffry D. Wert, Gregory F. Michno, John S. Gray, Nathaniel Philbrick James Donovan and Richard Allan Fox, Jr., all of whose books are found in our select bibliography. Their works are widely different, from monograph to biography to archeological analysis, and their conclusions are emphatically not the same. We will not attempt here to unveil the mysteries, surrounding that last hour, but rather to present a brief description of what may have transpired. We hope that it will be enough to pique your interest in pursuing the controversy through the vast Custer bibliography.

Historians believe that Custer had every expectation of being reinforced at any moment by Benteen's battalion and the pack train. Since Indian pressure was light at 4 p.m., he probably thought that he still had time to explore the possibility of capturing the women and children fleeing north from the camp by sending the Yates wing down to the Little Bighorn along Medicine Tail Coulee in a feint that would also draw Indians away from Reno, while he rode with the Keogh wing northeast to the broken ground known as the Nye-Cartwright Ridge. From that high point, he would be able watch his back trail for Benteen and assess Yates' progress. (There is speculation that the right wing, looking for a possible ford, also moved down toward the river below the area that is now the National Monument Headquarters and the National Cemetery.) Neither wing seems to have crossed the river. (Both movements were most likely feints to reduce pressure on Reno or on troops in his own battalion.) Under increasing pressure from warriors attacking from several directions, Armstrong now moved up the east rim of Deep Coulee to reunite with Yates at what is presently the southeast corner of the Little Bighorn Battlefield National Monument and would now be forced to fight in terrain, unfavorable for defense, that favored Indian infiltration of his positions. Sometime just after 4:00 p.m., Armstrong formed his battalion into a loose defensive box anchored on low ridges and high points inside the boundaries of what is now the National Battlefield Monument. However, his men were too few and their enemy too numerous, well-armed and skillful to be held at bay for long.

When it began, the collapse of the 7th's position proceeded rapidly. Crazy Horse, an Oglala Sioux, led a group of warriors westward across Custer Ridge, isolating the troops holding Calhoun Ridge. Troop C advanced down Calhoun Coulee in an effort to counter infiltrators, but was itself routed. That rout spread until the surviving troopers retreated in panic back toward Custer Hill. Other warriors were able to flank the troopers thrown out in a thin skirmish line to the southwest of Custer Hill (now known as the South Skirmish Line.) Many members of the Gray Horse Troop, the scout, Mitch Boyer, and regiment surgeon Dr. George E. Lord died on that slope. The three Custer brothers, their nephew, Armstrong "Autie" Read, and some 39 other officers and men of the 7th Cavalry (15 of the grave markers located there are thought to be spurious) met their deaths on Custer Hill. In the end, it was a massacre, with mounted warriors circling the dismounted cavalrymen while shooting them down, occasionally dismounting to "count coup" on a helpless or wounded trooper before dispatching him with a knife or club. Curley, the 17-year-old Crow scout whom Custer had earlier released from duty, stopped to look back from a vantage point a mile and a half to the east. Years later he remembered that the gunfire was continuous, "like the snapping of the threads in the tearing of a blanket."

Deep Coulee (Photo: Dave Taylor)

In their frenzy of victory, Indian women stripped the dead of their clothing, mutilated their corpses, and left them to lie where they fell, all, that is except Armstrong. Kate Big Head, a Cheyenne woman who had been taken prisoner after the Washita battle, claimed many years later that two Cheyenne women had prevented Armstrong from being mutilated because of his one-time union with Monahsetah, the daughter of the Cheyenne chief, Little Rock.

Weir Point (Photo: Dave Taylor)

Benteen and Reno had made a half-hearted effort to come to Armstrong's aid, if they even thought he was actually in need of their aid. Alarmed at the sound of distant gunfire and apparently on his own volition, Capt. Thomas B. Weir had independently left Reno Hill with his Company D just before 4:00 p.m. in an effort to locate Custer's battalion. He halted at a high point (now known as Weir Point) a mile or so to the north of Reno Hill where both Benteen and Reno caught up with him at 5:30 p.m. (Reno was delayed by the 20 minutes he spent recovering the body of his slain adjutant, Lt. Benjamin Hodgson.) In any case, it was too late; by the time they reached Weir Point, Custer's battalion was in its death throes. For a time, they could hear random gun fire coming from a hill to their north, but they could make out little because of the dust being raised by milling horses.

Then, the firing died out and they could see mounted warriors moving their direction. That sight prompted Benteen to leave with his company without informing Weir of his intention. Reno did the same. Abandoned, without senior leadership and facing an Indian horde, Weir withdrew to Reno Hill as well.

The surviving cavalrymen formed a defensive perimeter on Reno Hill, digging shallow rifle pits in anticipation of the attack they knew was imminent. Indian attacks began in the late afternoon of the 25th and continued sporadically through the night only to be renewed again in earnest the next day. In this desperate situation, Frederick Benteen came to the fore, striding upright between the rifle pits, encouraging his men and bringing some order to the still-panicked men in Reno's battalion. By all accounts, Marcus Reno, nominally the senior commander, was merely a cipher.

Through the night, troopers were continually moving down to the river with kettles and buckets to bring water back to their parched comrades; twenty were later awarded the Congressional Medal of Honor for their courage (four additional men who fought on or near on Reno Hill were also awarded the Medal for bravery not connected to the water details.)

Then, in mid-afternoon on the 26th, Indian gunfire died out as the beleaguered troopers watched as the enormous Indian camp and pony herd, obscured in a cloud of dust and smoke from a prairie fire, moved south along the far side the Little Bighorn, never to be seen (or even exist) again. The Terry-Gibbon column's appearance from down river shortly thereafter explained this sudden exodus.

The sight and smell of some 200 mutilated corpses strewn across the battlefield must have come as a shock to the new arrivals as well as to the Reno/Benteen survivors. Almost immediately, the grisly job of identifying and burying the dead fell to burial details. Many of the bodies were mutilated beyond recognition. The details lacked the shovels and picks as well as the psychological strength for the task; they were slipshod in both identification and burial. Most of the corpses were never identified and often they appear to have been hastily buried by covering them with soil scooped from two shallow trenches dug on either side. As a result, determining the exact location and number of gravesites has plagued researchers ever since.

It took the better part of five days to move the 43 wounded men downstream to Captain Grant Marsh's *Far West*. The steamboat got underway in the morning of July 3 and reached the hospital at Bismarck on the 5th. Terry's report of the disaster at the Little Bighorn was telegraphed from Bismarck late that evening. The *Far West* also carried a letter from Gen. Terry addressed to the acting commander of the fort. After reading it, Capt. William S. McCaskey gathered up a handy aide and the post surgeon and walked to the Custers' quarters where he broke the news to the saddened wives gathered there. Libbie, ever the brave and loyal Army wife, masked her grief and began to pay sympathy calls on the 24 other officers' widows in her capacity as the wife of their commanding officer.

Comanche

"Comanche" was an army horse purchased in 1867 by Capt. Myles Keogh for his personal use in battle. Although wounded during a running fight with Comanche warriors that year, the bay (or claybank) gelding stayed on his feet, carrying Keogh safely through the fight — hence his name.

Somehow Comanche, although severely wounded, survived the Battle of the Little Bighorn. He was found on the battlefield two days later, loaded with the rest of the wounded on the *Far West* for the dash downriver to Bismarck and Fort Lincoln where he was nursed back to health.

Col. Samuel Sturgis signed General Order #7 on April 11, 1878 calling on the 7th Cavalry to give special consideration to

Comanche. "Wounded and scarred as he is," Sturgis' Order read, "his very existence speaks in terms more eloquent than words, of the desperate struggle against overwhelming numbers, of the hopeless conflict and the heroic manner in which all went down that fatal day."

Comanche moved with the 7th to Fort Meade and then to Fort Riley, Kan. By then, he was a regimental pet, leading parades and guzzling beer.

He died on November 7, 1891 and was given a military funeral, the first Army horse to be so honored. Instead of being simply buried, however, he was mounted by a University of Kansas taxidermist and put on display at the University's Natural History Museum. He is still there despite several efforts over the past century to display him elsewhere. Ten years ago, the museum staff restored Comanche and made him the centerpiece of a new exhibit. He was probably not the only cavalry horse to survive the ill-fated battle, but he is the only one for which we have provenance.

The University of Kansas Natural History Museum is located on the Lawrence campus in Dyche Hall. It is open 9 a.m. to 5 p.m., Tuesday through Saturday, and from 12 p.m. to 4 p.m. on Sunday. It is closed on Mondays and major holidays. Phone: (785) 864-4450.

The University campus can be accessed from I-70 after you clear the greater Kansas City area to the west.

AFTERMATH

Libbie was determined not to let the memory of her fallen husband be forgotten. Despite criticism of Custer in the aftermath of the battle, she worked to keep his flame burning brightly. By the end of 1876, she was actively assisting pulp fiction writer and Civil War veteran, Frederick Whittaker, as he assembled his laudatory biography, published the following year. In the years that followed, she paid off the debt she was saddled with by her husband's death, wrote articles and went on lecture tours glamorizing Autie and the life they shared. Libbie never remarried, spending her remaining life between New York City and Florida. Her greatest contributions to the Custer legend and to history are found in her three books: "Boots and Saddles" (1885); "Tenting on the Plains" (1887); and "Following the Guidon" (1890.) As long as she lived, the flattering portrait she drew of her late husband and their life together went largely unchallenged. She died on April 4, 1933, just short of her 90th birthday and lies next to her Autie in the United States Military Academy Cemetery at West Point.

Finding Custer at the Little Bighorn Battlefield National Monument, Crow Agency, Mont.
The Battlefield, located on the Crow Indian Reservation, can be accessed from I-90 at Exit 510 (Crow Agency) or from State Highway 212 if you follow the 7th Cavalry's route from the Yellowstone River. The entrance to the National Monument is a mile east of I-90 and is clearly marked.

There are no camping facilities inside the Monument. In addition, federal law prohibits the removal or disturbance of any artifact, marker, relic or historic site. Watch for rattlesnakes if you hike the trails in the warmer months.

After paying the rather complicated entrance fee, your first stop should be the Visitor Center/Museum/Bookstore. Pause long enough to view the 25-minute orientation film, before exploring the bookstore, with its large collection books about Custer and western history, and the museum that contains exhibits depicting Armstrong's life (including one of his West Point uniforms), period weapons and Indian artifacts—many of which were found on the battlefield. Try to time your visit so that you can take in one of the informative overviews of the battle given by Park Service personnel at 10 a.m., 1:00 p.m. and 3:00 p.m. (depending on the season and weather) on the porch behind the Center.

Next to the Visitor Center are several acres of veterans' graves filling the Custer National Cemetery. Many Indian Wars veterans rest here, including Maj. Marcus Reno (reburied here in 1967), Capt. William Fetterman of Fetterman Massacre infamy, four Crow scouts who rode with the 7th Cavalry – (White Swan, Goes Ahead, Curley and White-Man-Runs-Him) – as well as soldiers from more modern times. From the Cemetery, walk up to Last Stand Hill and the 7th Cavalry Memorial and the newer Indian monument.

The present granite obelisk atop Custer Hill dates from 1881 – it replaced an earlier wooden one – and bears the names of the men of the 7th Cavalry who were killed during the battle, including those of Custer, his two brothers, Tom and Boston, and a nephew, Armstrong (Autie) Reed, misidentified as Arthur Reed. The remains of all the dead troopers that could be located at that date lie underneath. Some of their names appear on the steles, white-marble tablets, found on the hillside below the obelisk and scattered around the battlefield. (Custer's name is highlighted and turned so that someone standing near the Monument can easily read it.) Others tablets mark unidentified graves.

Memorial marker where some 220 soldiers, scouts and civilians were reburied in 1881. (Photo: Dave Taylor)

The story behind the placing of those tablets is both interesting and confusing; the confusion even greater now as similar red marker tablets commemorate fallen Indian warriors.

With help from men assigned from Terry's column, survivors of the battle dug the first graves where their comrades had fallen. Wooden stakes marked the sites. Not satisfied, the Army sent two details, one in 1877 and another in 1879, to improve the gravesites. The 1877 detail also exhumed the bodies of officers so they could be reburied according to their families' wishes.

Headstones where soldiers fell. (Photo: Dave Taylor)

The story behind the placing of those tablets is both interesting and confusing; the confusion even greater now as similar red marker tablets commemorate fallen Indian warriors.

With help from men assigned from Terry's column, survivors of the battle dug the first graves where their comrades had fallen. Wooden stakes marked the sites. Not satisfied, the Army sent two details, one in 1877 and another in 1879, to improve the gravesites. The 1877 detail also exhumed the bodies of officers so they could be reburied according to their families' wishes.

When a later 1881 detail exhumed the remains of the dead troopers for reburial under the Monument, it marked the original gravesites with wooden markers, which remained in place (or not, as the wind and weather dictated) until 1890 when Capt. Owen Sweet marked 246 former gravesites with the marble tablets you see today. But, there is a problem. Sweet included 44 marker tablets for those men killed in the Reno/Benteen fight, in addition to the 202 for those who rode with Custer. Then, for some unknown reason, caretakers at the site later added another six marker tablets.

Today, according to archeologist Richard A. Fox, Jr., there are some 42 extra marble tablets. That number is only a close approximation since we are not absolutely certain of the number of cavalrymen who died at the Little Bighorn. Further, they do not represent with any certainty the places where those men fell.

The Indian marker tablets are more recent. Problematic contradictions exist. Since 1999, five red granite tablets have been sited to mark places where a Sioux or Cheyenne brave "Died in Defense of His Homeland." They are not burial sites because neither tribe buried its dead and further, the Crow nation claims this area as its homeland and views the other tribes as transients and interlopers.

Indians tribes have also placed a memorial on the north slope of Custer Hill consisting of black wire sculptures of three mounted horsemen with a woman running beside them. They represent warriors riding to defend their village.

The Indian memorials have come about as a result of Federal legislation passed in 1991— and signed by then President George H. W. Bush. The legislation also authorized the name change from the Custer Battlefield to the Little Bighorn Battlefield.

Although the National Park Service, which has administered the battlefield since 1940, has blocked reenactments on the actual battlefield, two rival pageants are held each year on June 25th, the anniversary of the "Last Stand." One, staged annually since 1964, is presented by the Crows and is based on a script written by Joe Medicine Crow, a UC-Berkeley trained anthropologist. The rival reenactment is put on by the Real Bird family of the Crow tribe near the river where the Indian camp was located in 1876; it is reputed to be much less scripted.

So again, Custer, Crazy Horse and all the earnest warriors of both sides do battle — this time for the edification of the tourists who flock to the battlefield each year.

As Indian activist and writer Vine Deloria, Jr. once reminded us, "Custer Died for Your Sins," but Armstrong's memory certainly lives on.

To more fully explore the battlefield, there are several options available:

- The Park Service brochure given to you at the entrance gate will guide you along a multi-stop, self-guided automobile tour covering the 4.5 miles of the battlefield.
- The Park Service has also created a "Cell Phone Audio Tour" of the battlefield that runs 1.5 hours. Details are available at the Visitor Center.
- You can also purchase an hour and twenty-minute Auto Tour DVD with commentary by battlefield archeologist Richard Fox if you have a mobile device that can display it (or view it as a reminder of your visit when you return home.)
- Apsaalooke Tours runs buses from the Visitor Center hourly from 10 a.m. to 3 p.m. daily. The tours last an hour during which you will be accompanied by a Native American guide. Reasonably priced tickets can be purchased at the Visitor Center front desk.

The battlefield itself is remarkably preserved, including the ridgeline east of the river where Custer and his men, along with Sioux and Cheyenne warriors, rode, fought and died despite its running parallel to private land holdings. A visitor is struck by the ravines and steep riverbanks that made fighting and visibility so difficult here. Only the blacktop road, the stele tablets and the modern Visitor Center and Cemetery mar the pristine view.

Painting depicting Last Stand in Visitor's Center (Photo: Dave Taylor)

Finding Custer Near the Little Bighorn Battlefield
Garryowen, Mont.

Visitors can experience a different kind of museum and monument five miles south of the Little Bighorn battlefield at the "town" of Garryowen. The Custer Battlefield Museum contains a new exhibit centered on the only known photograph of Crazy Horse, the famous Oglala Sioux chief.

Christopher Kortlander, who formerly operated a California-based collectibles business, bought the entire town of Garryowen in 1993. He registered the Custer Battlefield name when the U.S. government changed the name of the National Monument to the Little Bighorn Battlefield National Monument.

The town was originally founded by the Burlington

Northern Railroad and named for the 7th Cavalry's famous marching song.

It was near present-day Garryowen that Maj. Reno's command began its attack against the Indian camps in the valley of the Little Bighorn.

"Burying the hatchet" at the Little Bighorn Battlefield in 1926 (Photo: Christopher Kortlander)

Another of Garryowen's interesting features is the Battle of the Little Bighorn monument that displays busts of Custer and Sitting Bull flanking the tomb of an "unknown soldier," a 7th Cavalry trooper whose remains were found years later. Exactly 50 years after the battle, White Bull, a Minneconjou Sioux Chief, and Gen. Edward S. Godfrey dedicated the tomb, while Col. J. M. T. Partello and Chief Red Tomahawk dropped a tomahawk and some tufts of native grass into the grave, giving real meaning to the expression, "burying the hatchet."

Garryowen, located off of Interstate 90's Exit 514, consists of a museum, rest stop, gas station, sandwich shop, convenience store and information center. The town and its museum are certainly worth a visit. Phone: (406) 638-1876; or visit the website at: www.custermuseum.org .

Nearby:
Jill and Putt Thompson's **Custer Battlefield Trading Post** is located across the road at the entrance of the National Monument. The trading post offers great Indian tacos and other food, beadwork, posters, Custer memorabilia and other gifts. Phone: (406) 638-2270; www.laststand.com.

The Crow Tribe operates the **Apsaalooke Nights Casino** just outside the entrance to the National Monument that may be a good place to park adult family members who would rather play the slots than tour the battlefield. Open daily 9 a.m. to 3 a.m. Summer; 10 a.m. to 2 a.m. Winter. Junction of I-90 and Hwy #212, Exit 510. 71 Heritage Road, Crows Agency, Mont. Phone: (406) 638-4440.

Accommodations near the Little Bighorn Battlefield
The closest town is Hardin, Mont. (population 3,500), about 11 miles north off I-90. Billings, another 45-minute drive west of Hardin, is Montana's largest city with a population of over 155,000. If you are heading south on I-90, the closest town is Sheridan, Wyo. (population around 17,500), about an hour's drive away. Consult hotel and restaurant websites for current information on accommodations and watering holes.

Despite its small size, according to TripAdvisor reviewers, Hardin boasts of a number of very good restaurants. Of course, the choice of accommodations and restaurants will be much broader in Billings and Sheridan.

The Buffalo Bill Center of the West, Cody, Wyo.

The Center, with its five museums and research library, is absolutely unique and should not be missed by anyone interested in the Custer saga. The museums, connected by a central rotunda, are the Cody Firearms Museum, the Whitney Gallery of Western Art, the Plains Indian Museum, the Buffalo Bill Museum and the Draper Museum of Natural History.

The **Mustang Grill/Pony Expresso** coffee bar, located on the main level, serves food and drink. A well-stocked gift shop and bookstore round out the facilities.

Your admission ticket is good for two days, so plan on seeing the museums in two or more sessions on different days. Your feet and back will demand it.

An alcove in the **Whitney Gallery of Western Art** is devoted to the "Battle of Many Names," as it styles the conflict on June 25, 1876. The Gallery exhibits three paintings depicting the battle by Edgar S. Paxson, N. C. Wyeth and W. Herbert Dunton. In the alcove, you can also find a portrait of Custer and a scene of the 7th Cavalry on the march.

The **Cody Firearms Museum** has carefully preserved examples of the types of guns used in the battle in its "The Plains Wars, 1866-1890" case.

The **Buffalo Bill Museum** has a pair of lithographs dealing with the battle and its reenactment as part of Buffalo Bill's "Wild West" show.

Pick up a copy of the "Finding Guide" in the "Battle of Many Names" alcove for the locations of other Custer memorabilia.

While children may not be interested by some of the museums, the two devoted to **Natural History** and the **Plains Indians** will fascinate them.

The Center of the West is located at 720 Sheridan Ave. It is open all year with hours varying by the season. An on-site, two-day admission ticket for adults is $19, with reduced rates for seniors, students and youths. Group rates are also available. Admission prices are slightly less if purchased online.

For further information and other opening times and dates contact the Center at: Phone: (307) 587-4771 or visit its website at www.centerofthewest.org.

Cody, located about 21 miles due east of Yellowstone National Park, can be reached from the Park and from both I-90 and I-94. Probably the most spectacular route leaves I-90 just north of Sheridan, Wyo. (Exit 9) and takes you through the Big Horn Mountains on Alternate State Highway 14. The view as you look west from the top of the pass into the Bighorn River valley is simply awesome.

Cody, Wyoming accommodations:
Today, Cody is a fully-developed tourist destination, with many motels, a **KOA Campground** and restaurants to accommodate the traveler. Sheridan Avenue, which leads to the center of town, is lined with interesting shops, motels and the **Historic Irma Hotel**, built by Buffalo Bill in 1902. The Irma stages "free gunfights" at 6 p.m. daily, except Sunday.

Finding the Rosebud Battle Site
The Rosebud Battlefield
To reach the Rosebud Battlefield from the Little Bighorn Battlefield, drive east on Highway 212 for 25 miles to Busby. Just before reaching Busby, Highway 212 makes a junction with Highway 314. Turn onto 314 and drive south along Rosebud Creek 25 miles to the turnoff to the Battlefield.

The state of Montana has indifferently marked this site, but there are signs at the turnoff from Highway 314 directing you west toward the Battlefield. After traveling a mile and a quarter on a gravel road, you reach a turnout with a toilet facility and a few picnic tables. Plaques nearby describe the battle, but they are so weathered as to be almost illegible. A stone monument stands a little farther on erected by the Bighorn County Historical Society in 1968. Rosebud Creek, here flowing almost due east, is on private land; there is a ranch house visible from the turnout. You can hike up a long meadow toward the initial Indian position, but the usual rattlesnake warnings apply. It is at least a quarter of a mile to the ravine where Crazy Horse's warriors were hiding.

If you continue south from the Rosebud Battlefield turnoff on Highway 314, you can approximately retrace the route in reverse that Gen. Crook took in June 1876. Highway 314 joins I-90 just north of Sheridan, Wyo., a town with excellent motels and restaurants.

Custer's Officers Were a Varied Lot

Many of the officers who served with Custer in the 1876 campaign had interesting backgrounds.

First Lt. William W. Cooke, Civil War veteran and Custer's Adjutant, hailed from Hamilton, Canada, where Grand Army of the Republic Post 472 was later named for him. First Lt. Charles DeRudio, né Carlo Camillo Di Rudio, was born to an aristocratic Italian family. He was convicted in an attempt to assassinate French Emperor Louis Napoleon, sentenced to and then escaped from Devil's Island before immigrating to America where he enlisted in the Union Army under the name of Charles DeRudio. He was promoted to 2nd Lt. in the U.S. Colored Infantry in 1864 and was with Reno's battalion on June 25th, so was fortunate to survive the battle. Capt. Tom Custer, who won two Medals of Honor during the Civil War, was killed not far from his brother, Armstrong; they were first buried in a shallow grave together.

Second Lt. James G. Sturgis, son of Col. Samuel Sturgis, commander of the 7th Cavalry and for whom the city of Sturgis, S.D. is named, died at the Little Bighorn; his remains were never identified. First Lt. Donald McIntosh, born in Canada to an Iroquois mother, commanded G Co. He was killed as Reno's attack collapsed and was later reburied in Arlington National Cemetery. Captain Myles W. Keogh, an Irishman who commanded I Co., once served in the Papal Zouaves, and died at the Little Bighorn, as did 2nd Lt. John Crittenden of L Co., son of Gen. T. L. Crittenden, Commanding Officer of the 17th Infantry. At his father's request, Crittenden's remains were buried where he fell.

LEGACY

So, after almost 140 years of examination and controversy, what are we to make of the legacy of George Armstrong Custer — heroic Indian fighter, precocious "Boy-General" or vain, headstrong, egotistical, martinet? The answer may depend on how attuned you, the reader, are to the socially, politically and environmentally correct opinions prevalent today. Wherever you stand, it's hard to be sympathetic with a 19th century American culture that drove indigenous peoples onto miserably inadequate reservations, while making extinct the multitudinous flocks of passenger pigeon and nearly inflicting the same fate on the vast herds of American bison. But, we must remember that Armstrong was a man of his time and that we are all caught in that analogous predicament today. To blame Custer for the sins, even some of them, of 19th century America, is absurd, despite social activist Vine Deloria's admonition that he symbolically died for our sins.

In the 1930s, the popular view of the heroic Custer embodied in the barroom reproductions of "Last Stand" paintings and Libbie's carefully crafted image of her husband crumbled rather rapidly. Frederic Van de Water's "Glory-Hunter: A Life of General Custer" appeared in 1933 before Libbie was settled in her grave at West Point next to her husband. Since that time, the tsunami of books, films and articles questioning his character and military talents has never really ceased. Armstrong's name was removed from his most famous battlefield in 1991. The Federal government has sanctioned and disbursed large monetary payments (e.g., $105 million to the Sioux in 1980) to Indian tribes for the land grabs it permitted and for which the name "Custer" has come to symbolize. Federally funded sites have sprung up, such as the memorial to the victims of the Sand Creek massacre in Colorado (probably mislocated due to Native American intransigence,) that memorialize the 19th century Indian rather than the white settler so often massacred by the Indian. At this moment, there is a proposal that the State of Colorado allow a rather macabre sculpture of a Cheyenne woman pleading for her child's life at Sand Creek be placed on the State Capitol lawn to commemorate that tragic event.

Despite all this revisionist activity, interest in Custer and his deeds, especially in the 1876 campaign, remains unabated. Books, articles and guidebooks such as this one continue to pour off the presses. Celebrations of events in Custer's life continue to be held from Michigan to Nebraska to Montana. Within the past decade, the National Park service has erected a modernistic building to commemorate the Battle of the Washita. (Although one suspects that the commemoration of the Battle was done more to placate Native American activists than to honor Custer and the 7th Cavalry.) Between 300,000 and 400,000 visitors annually pass through the gates of the Little Bighorn Battlefield National Monument. Custer ranks with Gens. Washington, Lee, Grant, Sherman, Eisenhower and Patton as the most widely recognized of American military figures, greatly surpassing his more successful Indian fighting contemporaries — Ranald Mackenzie, Nelson Miles, George Crook and Oliver Howard.

Possibly today's heroic view of Custer at the Little Bighorn stems from the Hollywood cavalry trilogy of director John Ford, "Fort Apache," "She Wore a Yellow Ribbon" and "Rio Grande," starring John Wayne, Ward Bond and Henry Fonda among other famous actors of the 1950s. However, more recent films have portrayed the post-Civil War military in a much less flattering manner, e.g., "Little Big Man" and "Dances with Wolves."

Whatever the truth of the Washita and Little Bighorn battles, Custer's name resonates with Americans today as the leader of a small heroic band fighting against insurmountable odds, similar to the Marines under Col. James Devereux and Cdr. Winfield S. Cunningham at Wake Island in 1941 or the Spartans under Leonidas at Thermopylae in 480 BC.

George Armstrong Custer still remains an enduring, if controversial, figure in America's epic western experience.

APPENDICES

1. PLAINS FORTS ASSOCIATED WITH THE CUSTERS

Of all these sites, probably the most rewarding to visit are Fort Hays, Fort Larned, Fort Abraham Lincoln and the Washita Battlefield National Monument. Fort Hays and the Washita NM are relatively easy to access from Interstates 70 and 40. Visiting Fort Larned will take a little more effort, but can be reached from either Hays or Dodge City, Kan. in about an hour's drive. Fort Larned, in addition to its completeness and relative isolation, let you easily drift back to its 19th century heyday.

Fort Abraham Lincoln State Park, N.D.

Fort Abraham Lincoln, built in 1872, was home to the 7th Cavalry, along with nearby Forts Rice and Totten. Armstrong took command of the 7th in 1873 and, after a month's stay in Monroe, he and Libbie called Fort Lincoln home for the remainder of his life. On February 6, 1874, their quarters burned down due to a chimney fire, destroying Libbie's wardrobe, but sparing Autie's uniforms. Fire also destroyed the building that replaced the original one. The house standing today is a reconstruction, built in 1989 for North Dakota's Centennial celebration.

It was from Fort Abraham Lincoln that Gens. Terry and Custer at the head of the 7th Cavalry marched for the Little Bighorn, with the sounds of "Gary Owen" echoing across the prairie.

Today, Fort Abraham Lincoln lies in a State Park outside Mandan, N.D. It includes both cavalry and infantry barracks, blockhouses, the Custers' quarters and a reconstructed Mandan Indian village known as On-A-Slant Village. Guides in period costume conduct tours of the buildings, and guided horseback tours are offered.

The Park can be reached by taking Exit 153 south from Interstate 95 – just west of Bismarck.

From the Park, it is possible to reach the Fort Rice Historical Site by driving south along the west bank of Lake Oahe for about 30 miles on state Highway 1806.

Find more at www.fortabrahamlincolnstatepark.com and the especially useful www.realnd.com/fortlincolnmap.htm .

Fort Cobb, Okla.

Fort Cobb, named after Secretary of the Treasury Howell Cobb, was opened in October 1859 as a base from which to supervise the removal of Texas tribes to Indian Territory and provide them protection from marauding Plains Indian war parties. The U.S. Army abandoned the post during the Civil War, while Confederate troops only occupied it sporadically. Indians sacked the Fort in October 1862. Fort Cobb was reopened by the Army in 1868 and thereafter was commanded by Col. William Hazen. The Army closed Fort Cobb in March 1869 when it opened Fort Sill some 30 miles to the south.

Generals Sheridan and Custer rode into Fort Cobb in the evening of December 18, 1868 and remained there until January 1869. It was during this interval that the two Army officers had their dramatic confrontation with the Kiowa chiefs Satanta (Set'tainte, White Bear) and Lone Wolf. The 7th Cavalry left Fort Cobb on January 6 for the site of the new Fort Sill.

The site of the old fort is approximately one mile east of the present day town of Fort Cobb, but nothing remains visible. There are two markers in town commemorating the abandoned Fort, one alongside a downtown street and the other at the Caddo County Fairgrounds. Both located off State Highway 9, which also serves as the main street for the town. See the website www.fortwiki.com/Fort-Cobb.htm for a map locating the markers and photographs.

Fort Dodge, Kan.
Fort Dodge is another of those Army posts that was established before the Civil War to protect travel on the Santa Fe Trail. A Col. Gilpin established Fort Mann west of Dodge City in 1847. The Trail branched here as some hardy wagoners dropped south to the Cimarron River in present-day New Mexico to avoid facing the climb over Raton Pass if they continued west along the Arkansas River.

Reacting to Indian attacks along the Trail, the Army directed Maj. Gen. Grenville Dodge to reopen travel in 1865. Dodge's Kansas Volunteers opened the new fort, located between two fords across the Arkansas, in March 1865. In its first iteration the new fort consisted of adobe and sod dugouts located near the river. Unhappy soldiers began to refer to the encampment as "Fort Dodge" to mock the general who had brought them here. Later, the War Department gave its official sanction to the name.

In the summer of 1866, construction began on more permanent buildings — officers quarters, a hospital and storage facilities. Over the next two years, soldiers built additional structures out of locally quarried limestone. Some of these buildings remain on the site today, including the two-story commanding officer's quarters.

By 1880, Fort Dodge had served its purpose and part of the land surrounding the Fort was sold to various local speculators and homesteaders. The Army officially closed Fort Dodge in April 1882; later that year the last remaining soldiers were marched south to Fort Supply. The Interior Department sold off most of the land surrounding the Fort in 1889. The remaining buildings and the ground around them were deeded to the State of Kansas in January 1890 for the purpose of establishing an old soldiers' home. Fort Dodge is still in use for that purpose today, some 124 years later.

Fort Dodge is located a few miles east of Dodge City off state Highway 400, which is a continuation of Dodge City's main thoroughfare, Wyatt Earp Avenue. A small museum occupied an original storehouse near the entrance and is open Monday, Tuesday and Friday from 10 a.m. to 4 p.m. The post itself is open to the public from 7 a.m. to 10 p.m. The important buildings that can still be seen include the Custer House, (originally the commanding officer's quarters that is not open to the public,) the Pershing Barracks (the original 1867 hospital) and the chapel constructed in 1902. Scattered around the post are some 50 cottages that are home to retired veterans and a number of modern buildings that serve the medical needs of the residents.

Fort Harker, Kan.

The first Army post at this site was Fort Ellsworth, named after a Lt. Ellsworth, built in 1864 at the junction of the Fort Riley-to-Fort Larned road and the Smoky Hill Trail. This site was abandoned two years later in favor of another about a mile away. The new fort was named after Gen. Charles G. Harker, a Union officer killed during the Civil War Battle of Kennesaw Mountain.

Fort Harker was mostly completed by the summer of 1867, at which time the structures at Fort Ellsworth were razed and the land sold to speculators. The present town of Ellsworth, Kansas was thusly born.

In Jul 1867, the Union Pacific, Eastern Division tracks reached Fort Harker, cementing its importance as a supply depot for Army posts farther west. By the end of 1867, the Fort was comprised of some 75 buildings and a supply depot guarded by four companies of the 38th Infantry. During that same summer, cholera struck the garrison and associated civilians. It was speculated that the soldiers may have brought the disease from St. Louis where they had been previously stationed. Regardless of its origin, by the year's end the disease had claimed the lives of 46 soldiers out of 892 cases reported. The toll among civilians at the post was heavy as well.

For the remainder of its existence Fort Harker served principally as a supply depot, although Gen. Philip Sheridan established his command post there in 1868-69. And, in 1869 and 1870, the 7th Cavalry used the post as a jumping off point for its 1870 campaign. Its usefulness ended by the expansion of rail lines, the Fort was abandoned in 1872.

Today, the Ellsworth County Historical Society is responsible for the three remaining buildings – the Commanding Officer's Quarters, Junior Officers Quarters and the guardhouse that contains a small museum devoted to the history of both Forts Ellsworth and Harker as well as local history. Another building that served as a Junior Officers Quarters is now a private residence.

The Fort Harker Guardhouse Museum address is: 303 W. Ohio Street, Kanopolis, KA 67454. To reach Kanopolis, take either the 219 or 225 Exits from Interstate 70, and then drive south to the town of Ellsworth. Kanopolis is about three miles southeast of Ellsworth. The use of a GPS-enabled device is recommended if you are unfamiliar with the area.

The Museum is open November through March on Saturdays, 10 a.m. to 5 p.m.; Sundays, 1 p.m. to 5 p.m.; May through September on Saturdays, 10 a.m. to 5 p.m.; Sundays, Tuesdays and Fridays, 1 p.m. to 5 p.m.; April and October on Saturdays, 10 a.m. to 5 p.m., Tuesdays through Fridays and Sunday, 1 p.m. to 5 p.m. There is a small admission charge for adults and children over seven.

Fort Hays, Kan.
Fort Hays had its origin as Fort Fletcher, an Army post named after Missouri Governor Thomas C. Fletcher, established in October 1865 because of increasing Indian attacks along the Smoky Hill Trail. After the Butterfield Overland Dispatch Company failed in 1866, the Army closed the Fort and then, reopened it a year later because of the approach of the Union Pacific's Southern Division (soon to be renamed the Kansas Pacific) railroad. At that time, it was renamed Fort Hays. The original fort was virtually destroyed by a flash flood on nearby Big Creek in 1867 while Libbie Custer was a resident there. The Army then chose a new, 7,640- acre site closer to the railroad right-of-way and on higher ground for the new Fort Hays. The new fort served as a supply depot, as well as base for a number of Army units including the 7th and 10th Cavalry and 5th Infantry Regiments, for the duration of the Indian Wars. Closed in November 1889, the Fort was given to the State of Kansas in 1900 for the site of a proposed state college, an agricultural experimental station and a park. Today, the few remaining fort buildings lie on the edge of the grounds of Fort Hays State University and near the site of Kansas State University's agricultural experimental station.

Old Fort Hays now is a state historic site administered by the Kansas Historical Society. It consists of a new administration building that houses a small museum and gift shop, two of original frame buildings that served as officer quarters, a stone blockhouse and a low, stone building that served as a guardhouse. The Kansas Travel web page reproduces photographs of the buildings at: www.kansastravel.org/forthays.htm.

The site is open Wednesday through Saturday, 9 a.m. to 5 p.m. Admission is charged for adults and students. Children aged five and under and Kansas Historical Foundation members are admitted free.

The Fort Hays Historic Site is easily reached by taking Exit 157 off I-70 (just west of the city of Hays) and driving south on alternate Highway #183 for four miles. Phone: (785) 625-6812; email: thefort@ksha.org .

Fort Larned, Kan.

What a surprise it is to walk across the new bridge that spans the Pawnee Fork (now the Pawnee River) of the Arkansas River and step onto the parade grounds of Fort Larned. If you were expecting to see a couple of dilapidated old buildings left over from the 19th century, you will be disappointed. Instead, you are confronted with a group of seemingly untouched, mostly one-story sandstone-block buildings defining a central parade ground. Fort Larned is virtually intact (or, at least, the Fort's last iteration is virtually intact) because it remained in private hands from 1884 until 1964 when it became a National Historic Site, part of the National Park System. Only the blockhouse at one corner is a complete reconstruction.

Fort Larned was vibrant as an outpost on the Santa Fe Trail years before the post-Civil War Indian wars on the southern plains. Its first iteration was as the "Camp on Pawnee Fork," dating from October 1859. The original camp soon became known as "Camp Alert" and was soon moved west to its present location. The Army ordered a more substantial adobe fort built on the site that was named Fort Larned after Col. Benjamin F. Larned, the Paymaster-General of the Army at the time. Later, the uncomfortable sod and adobe structures were replaced by the present stone and timber buildings.

Fort Larned's administrative offices and museum are located in an old enlisted barracks building on the southeast side of the parade ground. We would advise you to spend the ten minutes or so to view the film on the history and significance of the Fort. The museum contains some unique artifacts, among them are a quiver and peace pipe-tomahawk that are thought to have been taken from the Indian camp that Gen. Hancock's command burned in 1867 or from the Washita Battlefield in November 1868. (While their provenance may be uncertain, their authenticity is not.) And, then there is the cavalry sword hanging unassumingly on a back wall. It belonged to 1st Lt. Frank D. Baldwin, 5th U.S. Infantry, who served two short tours of duty at Fort Larned in the 1870s. Baldwin belongs to that small, select group of Americans who has been awarded the Congressional Medal of Honor twice. For Baldwin, the first award came because of an action in Georgia in 1864 and the second, during the Indian Wars, for leading the rescue of two female captives despite his command being badly outnumbered by the marauding Indians.

You can enter the breezeways that run through the officers quarters to view the period-furnished rooms through glass partitions.

Since the Santa Fe Trail actually wound around the Fort, Park Rangers on duty can direct you to a nearby overlook from which you can see the ruts made by the thousands of wagons that passed by during the middle of the 19th century.

Fort Larned is host to a number of special events — on Labor Day weekend the Fort sponsors a living history event; including historical re-enactors; candlelight tours are held on the second Saturday in October; and, old-fashioned Yuletide celebrations are held on the second Saturday of December.

Fort Larned National Historic Site is located off Kansas Highway #156 just east of the town of Larned, which is about halfway between Hays and Dodge City. Great Bend is about 25 miles to the northeast on Highway #56. The Fort is open from 8:30 a.m. to 4:30 p.m. daily. Traveling a little out of your way to visit this site is certainly well worth the time and trouble. For the visitor's convenience, the Park Service has provided a picnic area at the entrance to the Fort's grounds.

Fort Leavenworth, Kan.

Fort Leavenworth is the oldest Army post west of the Mississippi River and has been in continuous use since its founding in 1827. In 1881, Gen. William T. Sherman of Civil War fame, designated Leavenworth as the home of the School of Application for Cavalry and Infantry that later became today's U.S. Army Command and General Staff College. Leavenworth is today also home to the U.S. Army Combined Arms Center. There are numerous monuments, sites and buildings of historical interest on the post.

Leavenworth is home to the Frontier Army Museum (100 Reynolds Ave. with its public entrance off Grant Ave.) The Museum holds an extensive collection of over 7,000 items relative to the history of the Fort and the Frontier Army. The Museum is open Tuesday – Friday, 9 a.m. to 4 p.m.; Saturday, 10 a.m. to 4 p.m.; closed Sundays, Mondays and national holidays. Phone: (913) 684-3191.

It is also the site of the Buffalo Soldier Memorial Park dedicated in 1992 by Gen. Colin Powell to honor the

African-Americans who served in all-black units in the Frontier Army.

The Post also contains one of the 12 National Cemeteries established by Abraham Lincoln. For readers of this guide, the cemetery is notable because it contains the grave of Capt. Thomas W. Custer, two-time winner of the Medal of Honor, who died with his brothers Armstrong and Boston at the Little Bighorn.

There are two suggested driving tours around the Fort's grounds: one of a general nature that has stops at 16 locations and a second tour that concerns the history of the Mormon Battalion that was organized during the Mexican War (1846-48.)

Of course, Fort Leavenworth is famous as the location for the U.S. Disciplinary Barracks, the oldest federal penal institution, established in 1875.

Fort Leavenworth is most easily accessed by leaving I-70 at Exit 224 toward Leavenworth-Bonner Springs. Enter the post through the Grant (Main) Gate at the corner of 7th Street and Metropolitan Avenue. Stay in the right lane as you approach the gate.

Those seeking to visit Fort Leavenworth must obtain a visitor's pass at the entrance. That will require showing current photo identification, automobile registration and proof of auto insurance. Visitors must stay buckled up and refrain from using cell phones while driving around the post and children must be in appropriate car seats.

Fort McPherson, Neb.

The Army established its first post here along the Overland Trail in the fall of 1863, naming it Fort McLean. Three years later, in 1866, the name was changed to Fort McPherson in honor of Maj. Gen. James B. McPherson, a Union general killed during the Battle of Atlanta (the second highest ranking Union officer killed in action during the Civil War.)

The Fort stood on a strategic spot on the Overland Trail and the proposed route of the Union Pacific Railroad, near the junction of the North and South Platte Rivers. In 1873, it was chosen for the site of a national military cemetery, so that when the Fort was abandoned and its buildings sold in 1880, the cemetery remains to mark the site.

Today, the Fort McPherson National Cemetery contains 3,700 gravesites including the remains of 63 black "Buffalo Soldiers" belonging to the 9th and 10th U.S. Cavalry Regiments and four Medal of Honor winners. The Cemetery is also the location of one of the 17 remaining Meigs Lodges, the one-and-a-half story Second Empire style structures designed by Quartermaster-General Montgomery C. Meigs found in Civil War era cemeteries.

The Fort McPherson Cemetery is located off Interstate 80 (Exit 190), 12 miles east of North Platte, Nebraska. The exit for the Fort McPherson National Cemetery is signed from the Interstate. The nearest town is Maxwell, Nebraska. It is open daily from dawn to dusk; the administrative building is open weekdays from 8 a.m. to 4:30 p.m., except for national holidays other than Memorial Day. Phone: (308) 582-4433. Additional information is available on the Department of Veterans Affairs website: https://www.google.com/?gws_rd=ssl#q=department+of+foreign+affairs+Fort+McPherson+Cemetery.

Fort Rice, N.D.

See the entry under Fort Abraham Lincoln listed above.

Fort Riley, Kan.

Fort Riley today is an active U.S. Army base that is home to the 1st Infantry Division. It is named for Maj. Gen. Bennett C. Riley who, in 1829, commanded the first Army detachment escorting travelers down the Santa Fe Trail. Construction of a fort (first named Fort Center) along the Kansas (Kaw) River began in 1853 and the post has been in continuous use since that date. The arrival of the Union Pacific Railroad in 1866 enhanced its importance in the coming campaigns against the southern Plains Indian tribes. Gen. Sheridan saved Riley from the fate of so many of the Kansas forts when he recommended, in 1884, that it become the Cavalry Headquarters and site of the U.S. Army Cavalry School. Those designations meant Fort Riley would not be abandoned and sold to speculators. Because of its long history, the Fort has much to offer the visitor today by way of museums, monuments and historic buildings.

Today, there are three major museums located at Fort Riley:

The U.S. Cavalry Museum and Vehicle Display. Open Monday through Saturday, 9 a.m. to 4:30 p.m. and Sunday, 12 p.m. to 4:30 p.m.

The Fort Riley 1st Infantry Division Museum. Open Monday through Saturday, 10 a.m. to 4 p.m. and Sunday 12 p.m. to 4 p.m.

The Custer House Museum. This is the museum that probably will be of the greatest interest to the readers of this guide. The Museum is located in one of the original officers quarters buildings, unfortunately not the one in which Autie and Libbie actually resided. Rooms are furnished with period pieces from the 1870s and 1880s. Open on Saturdays, 10 a.m. to 4 p.m., and Sundays, 1 p.m. to 4:30 p.m. from Memorial Day to Labor Day.

Call (785) 239-2737 for inquiries about the museums and their opening times.

The Fort Riley Reservation lies between Junction City and Manhattan north of Interstate 70. Leave the Interstate at Exit 301 (Riley-Marshall Field) and drive north to the post entrance. You will need to pick up a visitor's pass at the gate. At that time, you must show a photo ID, your car registration and proof of insurance. There may be restrictions on your movement within the post. Only U.S. citizens are permitted to visit Fort Riley.

Fort Sedgwick, Colo.
The Army built this post, originally Fort Rankin, on the south side of the South Platte River a mile upriver from Julesburg. It was renamed in September 1866 for Maj. Gen. John Sedgwick, a Union officer killed at the Battle of Spotsylvania Courthouse. The Fort served as a refuge for settlers during the Indian raids on Julesburg in 1865. The Army closed Sedgwick on 31 May 1871 and transferred the property to the Interior Department in 1884.

Fort Sedgwick is remembered by two roadside markers: one on south side of State Highway 136 just east of the town of Ovid; the other, marking the approximate site of the post hospital, is off CR 28, south of the town. This marker is just beyond the farm on the north side of the road. To reach it after you leave Interstate 76 at Exit 172, drive north on CR 29 (27.8) toward the town of Ovid. In less than a mile, turn east on CR 28, an unpaved road. The marker is just beyond the farm (about one-half mile) on the north side of the road. The Fort itself was located in the fields near the farm complex.

The Fort Sedgwick Historical Society maintains two museums in Julesburg: (1) The Depot Museum located in the old railroad station and housing artifacts from early pioneer life: and (2) a newer Fort Sedgwick Museum that has displays relating to the history of the post, a book store and administrative offices. The Fort Sedgwick Museum is open year-round, while the Depot Museum is open only in the summer.

Contact information: Fort Sedgwick Historical Society, 114 E 1st St., Julesburg, CO 80737. Phone: (970) 474-2061; email: history@kci.net .

Fort Sill, Okla.

Gen. Phil Sheridan personally picked the site for Fort Sill in January 1869 after he found the more isolated location of Fort Cobb deficient. Fort Sill, named after one of Sheridan's friends killed in the Civil War at the Battle of Stones River while mistakenly wearing Sheridan's coat, proved to be well located near the reservations in Indian Territory. The new post played a strategic part in both the Indian wars of the late 1860s and in the Red River War of 1874-75 that ended Native American resistance to the Federal Government's reservation policies on the southern plains.

Fort Sill has remained in active service since its founding, now serving as a basic training camp for new recruits and as the Army and Marine Corps' artillery school.

There are two important museums on the base: the Fort Sill National Historic Landmark and Museum and the U.S. Army Field Artillery Museum.

The Landmark Museum opened in 1935 and has expanded over the years to house over 235,000 artifacts utilizing 38 of the post's buildings, new as well as historic. In 2009, the Army opened the Field Artillery Museum as a separate entity and relocated artifacts relating to the history of artillery from the Revolution forward to the new building.

Fort Supply, Okla.

In November 1868, Gen. Alfred Sully marched five companies of the 5th Infantry to this spot in order to establish a supply base. Custer and the 7th Cavalry rode in from Fort Dodge at the end of the month and, and then used it as a base for their attack on Black Kettle's village on the Washita River. What was obviously at first intended to be a temporary base, Camp Supply was later moved a half mile to the southwest, where it proved to be conveniently located to support Army operations for the following 21 years. Renamed Fort Supply in 1889, the Army abandoned the post in 1893-94. Later, the buildings were used by the State of Oklahoma for a hospital.

Today, Fort Supply has been partly restored to reflect its 19th century importance. Unfortunately, it is located inside the grounds of the William S. Key Correctional Center, just east of the town of Fort Supply on Highway 183/270, and therefore, access is greatly restricted. However, it is open Tuesdays through Saturdays 9a.m. to 4p.m. by special appointment. Contact Mr. Shayne House at (580) 766-3767 at least 48 hours before your intended visit on the above days. There are excellent photographs of present day Fort Supply on the Santa Fe Trail Research website available at: http://www.santafetrailresearch.com/research/fort-supply-oklahoma.html.

Fort Wallace, Kan.

Fort Wallace was the Army's westernmost post on the Smoky Hill Trail and as such was a constant irritant to the southern Plains Indian tribes who frequented western Kansas. Gen. William T. Sherman authorized the Fort in October 1865 along with Forts Harker and Hays to extend the Army's reach from Fort Riley. Because of the lack of local timber and a decision to move the Fort to a more defensible location, construction lagged through the spring of 1867, when it was halted completely due to Indian attacks. Despite the fact that the post was home to some 544 soldiers that summer, construction could not be completed until 1870. The Fort's usefulness declined quickly in the next decade leading to the garrison's withdrawal in April 1882. The remains of soldiers buried in the fort cemetery were exhumed and moved to Fort Leavenworth. In 1886, local settlers began to dismantle the buildings and two years later another Homestead Act opened up the Fort's reservation to public entry.

Today, all that remains of Fort Wallace is the post cemetery with its civilian graves. A small museum and gift shop in nearby Wallace, Kansas commemorated the Fort, its garrison and local history.

To reach the site of Fort Wallace leave Interstate 70 at Oakley (Exit 76). After driving west through Oakley to State Highway 40, turn south for 45 miles to Wallace. The museum is just east of the town.

The Fort Wallace Museum is open in the summer 9 a.m. to 5 p.m., Monday through Saturday and 1 p.m. to 5 p.m. on Sunday. You are advised to call ahead before your visit. The museum's address is: The Fort Wallace Museum, Highway 40, Box 53, Wallace, KA 67761. Phone: (785) 891-3564.

Battlefield Site
Washita Battlefield National Historic Site, Cheyenne, Okla.

The administration building for the Washita Battlefield National Site is located just east of the town of Cheyenne, Okla., south of the valley of the Washita River. The National Park Service dedicated this striking and unusual building, which also houses the administrative offices of the Black Kettle National Grassland, in August 2007. In addition to administrative offices, the building is home to a small museum containing a fine collection of both U.S. Army and Indian artifacts. A very well done, 25-minute film, "Destiny at Dawn: Loss and Victory on the Washita," gives a relatively balanced account of the events that led up to the battle and of the battle itself. Viewing it is well worth the half-hour or so it will take out of your visit.

You can walk the battlefield itself by driving to an overlook a short distance west of the Administration Building. Well-kept trails, along with an invaluable trail guide available at the trailhead, make the tragic events of November 1868 come alive, especially when you stand on the spot where the Cheyenne pony herd was slaughtered. The bones of those 800-odd animals still covered the ground in 1935, when they were finally carted off for fertilizer. Various plaques, memorials and monuments are found nearby. The pavilion houses a restroom, water fountain and picnic tables.

The Visitor Center is open every day from 8 a.m. to 5 p.m., with the exceptions of Thanksgiving, Christmas and New Year's Days.

Trails are open daily from dawn to dusk.

Cheyenne sits astride state Highway 283, some 25 miles north of Interstate 40, which runs between Oklahoma City and Albuquerque. The exit from Interstate 40 is No. 20, 21 miles east of the Oklahoma-Texas border.

2. A NOTE TO MILITARY FIREARMS IN THE CUSTER ERA

The Evolution of the 1873 Springfield Rifle and Carbine
In 1872, the Army appointed a board to select a new rifle and carbine to replace the hodgepodge of weapons then in service use. This Ordnance Board, known as the Terry Board after its chairman, Gen. Alfred H. Terry, looked at some 109 various shoulder weapons before putting many of them through an exhaustive and somewhat quixotic series of tests for accuracy, reliability and durability. The Board quickly narrowed the field to 21 rifles from such manufacturers as Winchester, Springfield and Remington, to name three that later became famous. (Three rifles of foreign manufacture were also included in the group.) Then, the Board got down to what it considered serious testing.

In the absence of any clear doctrine to aid them in the selection of a service rifle to combat the Plains Tribes, the Board devised seven tests to rank the rifles as to their durability and reliability, only giving an afterthought to their possible tactical use. The *first* test was to fire damaged cartridges through each weapon. The *second* determined accuracy, the ability to strike a 6'x 2' board at 100 feet during rapid fire. A *third* test determined the rapidity of fire over a one-minute interval. The next, *fourth*, subjected each rifle to 500 rounds of sustained fire without cleaning. Then (hopefully after cleaning), *fifth*, each weapon was placed in a box where it was subjected to a two-minute blast of sand and dust, twenty rounds fired without cleaning, put back in the box for another two-minute blast and then fired another 20 times. *Sixth*, the rust test involved placing the rifles in an ammonia solution to the level of their chambers for ten minutes, and then exposing them to the air for two days before firing them 20 times. Finally, *seventh*, the weapons were tested with excessive loads, ending with rounds containing 90 grains of black powder. Samples of the rifles were also issued to troops in the field for real-life testing.

And, wouldn't you know it, the Board, which also counted Maj. Marcus Reno among its members, selected rifle number 99, a new variation of a rifle that had been in service use since the mid-1860s, a single-shot, trapdoor-action model that has come down to us as the U.S. Rifle, Model 1873, maybe better known as the Model 1873 Springfield.

The Springfield's lineage goes back to 1865 when the War Department asked the master armorer at the Springfield Armory, Erskine S. Allin, to develop a design for the conversion of the tens of thousands of Model 1861 and 1863 rifle muskets in the Federal inventory from muzzle-loading, percussion-cap weapons to breech-loaders firing modern metallic cartridges. Advised to disregard existing patents, Allin quickly came up with a workable design that involved cutting open the top of the breech of a rifle musket to accept a trapdoor-like breech block that opened via a hinge at its front. The external hammer now struck a firing pin running through the breech block to fire a rather underpowered .58 caliber, rim-fire cartridge.

The shortcomings of the first Allin conversion were immediately obvious and prompted its modification in 1866. The resulting rifle was not so much a new design as an improvement on the original. The .58 caliber barrels were reamed out and a .50 caliber rifled insert brazed inside. The redesigned rifle also chambered a powerful new rim-fire cartridge featuring a copper case loaded with 70 grains of black powder pushing a 450-grain bullet. The new rifles proved themselves in the Hayfield and Wagon Box fights in August of 1867, allowing the rapid fire of soldiers from the 27th Infantry to hold off sustained attacks by mounted Indians.

The rifle adopted by the Ordnance Board in 1873 was the fifth version of the Allin action, which advanced its original design in several ways. Newly manufactured steel barrels replaced the re-sleeved ones and were bored to .45 caliber. The new rifles chambered a powerful new round, the .45-70 Government (a 405-grain bullet driven by 70 grains of black powder in a copper, center-fire case.) The carbine version, issued to the cavalry, had a 10-inch shorter barrel and was chambered for the less powerful .45-55 round (loaded with 55 grains of black powder, held in place by a paper wad, instead of 70 grains.) Troopers of the 7th Cavalry fought with those carbines at the Little Bighorn.

It has been argued that what the Army needed in 1873 was not an improved single-shot rifle, but a repeater capable of rapid, sustained fire, possibly an improved version of the Spencer lever action rifle the 7th had carried into battle at the Washita River seven years before. Actually, a modern repeating rifle could have been included in the Army's tests, the Winchester Model 1873, later celebrated as "the gun that won the West." That rifle chambered a relatively weak (when compared to the .45-55) .44-40 round that could also be fired from a revolver such as the new Colt Single Action Army (New Model Army Metallic Cartridge Revolving Pistol,) also adopted in 1873. (Note: The Army's version of the Colt revolver was chambered for the more powerful .45 Long Colt.)

The Winchester '73 rifle was a direct descendant of the Winchester Magazine Rifle, Model 1866 and the even earlier Henry lever action rifle of 1860. The Winchesters differed in that they could be loaded through a port on the right side of the receiver directly into a closed, tubular magazine under the barrel, thus could be fired and reloaded without taking the weapon from the shoulder. The Winchester '73 could have provided just the sort of firepower the troopers of the 7th Cavalry might have put to good use at the Little Bighorn. To answer the critics who claim that the .44-40 round was not powerful enough, one can only say that the Spencer had served well enough at the Washita, less than a decade before, with a less powerful cartridge.

The Ordnance Board expressed its desire for a repeating rifle in its final report: "Resolved, that in the opinion of the Board, the adoption of magazine-guns for military service, by all nations, is only a question of time; that whenever an arm shall be devised which shall be as effective as a single breech-loader, as the best of the existing arms, and at the same time shall possess a safe and easily manipulated magazine, every consideration of public policy will require its adoption." The Winchester '73 might have been that rifle in 1876. Too bad it wasn't included in the 1873 round of tests.

We will never really how well the Springfield carbine served the troopers at the Little Bighorn. The Reno and Benteen battalions made good use of it in defending their position on Reno Hill and the weapon continued in service use for another 18 years, which suggests that the Army was not completely dissatisfied with it.

Archeological evidence from the battlefield has shown that there were a few cartridge cases (3.4%) that showed signs of having been pried from their chambers, suggesting that something like nine of the 200 plus carbines in the hands of the cavalrymen may have suffered extraction problems, but that carbine malfunction was not a widespread problem. (A somewhat higher percentage of pried .45-70 cases were found in Indian battle positions.) Whether the troopers under duress laid down effective fire with this single shot weapon is another question entirely, but archaeological evidence suggests that the reasons for Custer's debacle must be looked for elsewhere than malfunctions related to the Springfield carbine.

Custer himself carried a Remington sporting rifle firing a .50 caliber bullet from a brass case. Surveyors with metal detectors found several .50 brass cases scattered over the battlefield, indicating that other fighters present carried similar weapons.

Army Revolvers
The standard-issue revolver in use by the 7th Cavalry was the famous Colt Single Action Army (SAA) model, chambered for the .45 Long Colt cartridge. No one faults either the weapon or the cartridge, both of which, in modern versions, are still in production today. However, a sidearm of any model or caliber has always been of limited use on the battlefield because of its lack of accuracy except close range. Still, the number of .45 Colt bullets and cases found by archeological investigations shows that Colt SAA revolvers were fired repeatedly during the battle.

In 1875, the Army also approved the Smith & Wesson M1875 Army Schofield revolver for service use. It chambered the .45 Schofield cartridge that fired a 255-grain bullet. Battlefield shell-case recoveries show that some of these revolvers were also in use at the Little Bighorn.

Indian Weapons
The number and variety of modern firearms employed by the Sioux and Cheyenne warriors are astounding. Earlier finds, combined with the archeological survey of portions of the battlefield in 1984-85, have turned up cases and bullets from 28 different firearms, from cavalry weapons captured earlier in the fight (most likely carbines acquired during the Reno rout or even earlier at the Battle of the Rosebud) to obsolescent muzzle-loaders. The predominant repeating rifles in use were the Henry and Spencer lever-action models that had become available in the 1860s, but the Indians were also armed with numerous single-shot, .52 caliber, Sharps breech-loading rifles that had been adopted by the Army for limited issue in 1859. The earlier versions of this popular, but controversial weapon had employed a linen cartridge fired by a percussion cap. The newer version in

the hands of warriors at the Little Bighorn was chambered for a modern, .52 caliber, metallic cartridge. A few cases and bullets in .44-40 caliber, fired from Winchester '73s, also turned up, but were vastly outnumbered by those from the Henry and Sharps rifles. Firearms specialist Dick Harmon estimates that the warriors at the Little Bighorn battle possessed at least 192 repeaters, almost one for every cavalryman facing them. Those warriors were certainly not under-gunned and many carried bows as well.

For a more complete discussion of the firearms present at the Little Bighorn, see Dick Harmon's discussion in Douglas D. Scott and Richard A. Fox, Jr.'s, *Archaeological Insights into The Custer Battle: An Assessment of the 1984 Field Season* (University of Oklahoma Press, 1987.)

The Missing Gatling Guns
One of the persistent "what ifs" in the Custer saga involves his failure to take along the three available Gatling guns when he left the mouth of the Rosebud on his march to the Little Bighorn and it breaks into two speculations: 1) what if Custer had taken the guns along on his extended scout; and 2) what if he had been able to effectively employ them in his attack on the Indian camp.

The Gatling gun, the invention of Dr. Richard J. Gatling in 1862, was a cumbersome weapon at best. The multiple-barrels fired rounds from pre-loaded steel blocks that were loaded from a hopper. This loading system was prone to jam because of black powder fouling. The guns themselves were mounted on horse-drawn carriages that were not especially mobile. (Maj. Marcus Reno took one of the Gatlings along on his June 10-19 scout of the Tongue and Rosebud Rivers, only to have its carriage break down. He ordered the gun cached, but the officer commanding it managed to affect a repair and it continued on with the cavalry column.) The model available to Custer was most likely a six-barrel version firing a .58 caliber round at a maximum rate of 400 rpm. Custer, who did not think that they could keep up with his fast-moving cavalrymen, probably made the correct decision when he left the Gatlings behind, as he was well ahead of his pack train when he split his command prior to the attack on the Indian camps.

But, what if he had reached the battlefield with the Gatlings in tow? Those guns might have forced a change in Custer's tactics that alone might have staved off the ensuing disaster. One possible scenario has Custer deploying both his and Reno's troops as a single battalion along the valley floor route over which Reno actually attacked, with the Gatlings in supporting positions. With luck, the Indian warriors might have panicked or, at least, not been willing to launch a counterattack in the face of all that fire. But, more than likely, the Gatlings would have been back with the pack train and unavailable when the fight began. In any case, they were a non-factor at the Battle of the Little Bighorn.

Army Cannons

The Army also occasionally took the two-pounder Hotchkiss cannon on its Indian campaigns because it could be broken down and packed on the backs of three mules. Its 1.65-inch exploding shell was also accurate to a range of 4,000 yards. Gen. Nelson Miles tried to take it with him wherever he campaigned, only finding it a burden in Yellowstone Park, but other commanders thought artillery was useless on Indian campaigns. However, Light Battery E, First Artillery deployed four of these weapons at Wounded Knee in December 1890 with devastating effect.

The cannon taken on the Yellowstone Expedition are sometimes referred to as the "Rodman" cannon, but more likely they were 3-inch ordnance rifles, an extremely accurate weapon cast in Phoenixville, Pa. and the most numerous of the Civil war types. A true Rodman cannon was a much larger gun, cast using a water bath.

3. A FISTFUL OF FILMS ABOUT CUSTER

"Little Big Man" (1970)
"Son of the Morning Star" (1991)
"They Died With Their Boots On" (1941)

Well, to be precise, Gen. George Armstrong Custer is not the central character in all these films. **"Little Big Man"** actually follows the fictional picaresque life of the diminutive Jack Crabb, a/k/a Little Big Man, an 111-year-old "squaw man" who survived into the era of reel-to-reel tape recorders.

As Crabb, played by Dustin Hoffman, narrates his life to a condescending reporter, Armstrong appears in the narrative several times, most notably at the Battles of the Washita and the Little Bighorn, as the prototype for the brutal, culturally insensitive 19th century American westerner. Nothing in the film will help the viewer understand Custer or the Plains Indian Wars. It is obviously intended to be a parable (or maybe a satire, if you think either the director, Arthur Penn, or Hoffman had a satirical bone between them) on the Vietnam conflict and the cultural wars of the 1960s.

The Cheyenne, "the human beings" in the film's vernacular, are leading a peaceful, hippie lifestyle on the Great Plains, when into their paradise comes the white man, hell-bent on mayhem. Indian actor Chief Dan George, who plays Old Lodge Skins, the tribal guru and Little Big Man's foster grandfather, is symbolically blind and helpless as the 7th Cavalry begins its murderous attack at the Washita. And, that attack comes just after Little Big Man has enjoyed a little tipi sex with his wife's sisters and a friend while wife wanders off into the bushes to have their baby. Of course, the rampaging cavalrymen slaughter all the women, while the dismounted, and almost disembodied, regimental band stands in the snow mournfully playing "Gary Owen." At least that part of the scene is accurate; the band did play a few bars of the Irish drinking tune to signal the attack before their mouthpieces froze.

Years later, Jack Crabb found himself an unwilling participant at the Little Bighorn. But, the battle and Custer's demise are so poorly recreated as to be only symbolic of the fate awaiting all-arrogant American aggressors. All through the film, Armstrong has been little more than the stereotypical military-bad-guy.

Somehow, Hoffman, a method actor from LA, is a little hard to believe as Jack Crabb, a white orphan kid raised by the Cheyenne, who, like a 19th century Forrest Gump, was everywhere and seemingly met everyone in his tumultuous times, much less as Little Big Man, a Cheyenne brave. But, if you liked him as Tootsie, you'll probably love him as Little Big Man.

"Son of the Morning Star" is a film of another ilk – it affects pretensions to historical accuracy. The teleplay for the made-for-TV film, by Melissa Mathison, is based on Evan S. Connell's bestselling book and other sources, and therein lies the difficulty. Connell's "Son of the Morning Star" (1984) takes a few liberties with the Custer saga and we will never know what the "other sources" were. Although, given the film's emphasis on Crazy Horse, one suspects Stephen Ambrose's "Crazy Horse and Custer" (1975). Overall it is lamentable, because there are better sources than Connell for Armstrong's life and the 1876 Montana campaign.

Mathison cleverly uses dual narrators to carry the story along. A young Indian woman, Kate Bighead (Kimberly Norris, with voiceover by Buffy Sainte-Marie), gives the Indian perspective. She, like Little Big Man, just happens to be present at the critical moments in Armstrong's career. Second, Elizabeth (Libbie) Custer (Rosanna Arquette), wife of the General (Gary

Cole), provides the white, gentile perspective. The contrasting views and voices of the two women prove to be a useful cinematic construct. At the film's end, Kate can rationalize away the mutilation of Armstrong's body by some squaws as an acceptable cultural ritual, while Libbie agrees to help the post's surgeon break the news of their husbands' deaths to the wives at Fort Abraham Lincoln. Missing entirely are the voices of the thousands of Americans who were moving west in hopes of improving their lot.

The reenactment of the Battle of the Little Bighorn is staged about as well as it is likely to be. Enough of the elements are there to make the battle credible: Custer's non-regulation red kerchief and buckskins; his decision to attack the Indian camp without adequate reconnaissance; the fateful splitting of his forces; Capt. Frederick Benteen's perfidy; Maj. Marcus Reno's indecision and panic; sabers boxed and left behind before the final march; the straw hats some of troopers wore; and the Springfield carbines that jammed. Even the terrain where it was filmed looks much like the actual battlefield today. Only when the camera focuses periodically on the majestic and very distant Tetons does the reality of south-central Montana slip a bit, and reality slips further when the dead soldiers on Custer's Hill are shown with their hair and bodies intact, devoid of flies. But it is to be remembered that the film was shown first on prime-time TV and later rated PG.

Again, as in the other films reviewed here, the viewpoint is decidedly "politically correct." Custer and his command (with the exceptions of Benteen and Reno) are treated sympathetically, Crazy Horse and his Indian allies more so. Certainly we can all agree that the Indian wars of the 19th century were a national tragedy without indulging in historical self-flagellation. There are always multiple sides to every story and it's lamentable that movies/screenwriters can't offer a better telling. Maybe Benteen's reply to Gen. Terry's obvious question two days after the battle — "mistakes were made" — applies as well to the nation's failed Indian policy.

Quibbles aside, "Son of the Morning Star" provides a reasonably accurate and dramatic film rendition of Armstrong's life and the battle that ended it.

Warner Bros. studio did right thing by the Custer legend consistent with big Hollywood productions. **"They Died With Their Boots On"** cast two reigning heartthrobs, Errol Flynn and Olivia de Havilland, in their eighth and final film together. That alone ensures that Custer's life is portrayed as one long romantic tale, which in a way it was. There is no denying the real passion that Autie and Libbie brought to their 13-year relationship. Unfortunately, Flynn and de Havilland play the parts as if they had done it all before in their seven previous films, except for their final parting scene when they seem to know it will be their last together. Those were the days when Hollywood could effectively substitute décolletage and crinoline for sex; some of de Havilland's costumes look as if they were recycled from "Gone with the Wind."

Casting seems to have been a problem. Arthur Kennedy is fine as Custer's nemesis, Ned Sharp, but Anthony Quinn as Crazy Horse? In fact, executive producer Hal Wallis had trouble in recruiting Indian extras for the climactic battle scene; only 16 answered the call. Filipinos made up most of the Indian horde and were kept well in the background during the filming of the battle scenes.

Yet, the film projects a certain degree of realism, despite its California backdrop. So many of the extras and horses were injured in the battle scenes that it was necessary to set up a couple of field hospitals.

It's hard to be critical of a piece of 1941 fluff. "They Died With Their Boots On" is loosely based on Armstrong's life, i.e., he attends West Point, meets Libbie, fights in the Civil War, is promoted to brevet brigadier general, marries Libbie, goes West and dies heroically at the Little Bighorn. Almost everything else is fiction. Director Raoul Walsh later said that he tried to portray the Indian cause sympathetically, but mostly gets lost in the hail of arrows and bullets that doom Armstrong and his troopers at the Little Bighorn. "Little Big Man" is still 30 years off.

See the movie to enjoy Flynn and de Havilland in their final film flirtation and to enjoy a beery-besotted rendition of "Gary Owen" in an amusing bar scene, not to learn much about Autie, Libbie or the Little Bighorn.

Availability:
"Little Big Man" and "They Died With Their Boots On" are available on VHS tape and DVD. There is even a colorized VHS version of "They Died With Their Boots On." "Son of the Morning Star" is yet to be released on DVD, but a two-cassette VHS version is available.

BIBLIOGRAPHY

The list of published works on Custer and the Little Bighorn engagement seem endless. The very short bibliography that follows only mentions a few that seem especially valuable and insightful today.

Despite a hundred and thirty-nine years of criticism, Frederick Whittaker's laudatory biography in two volumes, "A Complete Life of General George A. Custer Vol. 1: Through the Civil War; Vol. 2: From Appomattox to Little Big Horn" (Sheldon & Co., 1876), written with the help of Libbie Custer, is still valuable as long as you understand its limitations. It is available in a modern reprint edition.

More recently, Jay Monaghan, "Custer: The Life of General George Armstrong Custer" (Little Brown, 1959); Robert M. Utley, "Cavalier in Buckskin: George Armstrong Custer and the Western Military Frontier" (University of Oklahoma Press, 1988); and Jeffry D. Wert, "Custer: The Controversial Life of George Armstrong Custer" (Simon & Schuster, 1996) all have written first-rate accounts of Armstrong's life. The older Stephen E. Ambrose's "Crazy Horse and Custer: The Parallel Lives of Two American Warriors" (Doubleday, 1975) develops an interesting comparison between the two adversaries.

Libbie Custer's three books, "Boots and Saddles; or, Life in Dakota with General Custer" (1885), "Tenting on the Plains; or General Custer in Kansas and Texas" (1887), and "Following the Guidon" (1890) helped keep the Custer myth alive well into the 20th century. All are available in reprint editions. Libbie's role in creating the Custer mystique is analyzed by Shirley A. Leckie in "Elizabeth Bacon Custer and the Making of a Myth" (University of Oklahoma Press, 1993). Libbie's life is the subject of Lawrence A. Frost's "General Custer's Libbie" (Superior Publishing Co., 1976). Armstrong himself wrote about his Kansas years in "My Life on the Plains; or, Personal Experiences with the Indians" (1874, New York, Sheldon & Co., University of Oklahoma Press reprint, 1976).

The best volume on Custer in the Civil War is Gregory J. W. Urwin, "Custer Victorious: The Civil War Battles of General George Armstrong Custer" (Associated University Presses, 1983).

The early Kansas years are carefully reconstructed by Minnie Dubbs Millbrook in her two articles in the *Kansas Historical Quarterly*, "The West Breaks in General Custer" (Summer, 1970) and "Custer's First Scout in the West" (Spring, 1973).

Concerning the Battle of the Little Bighorn, the studies are legion. We have found the following titles to be especially useful:

For the best traditional interpretation of the battle see Edgar I. Stewart's "Custer's Luck" (University of Oklahoma Press, 1955). John S. Gray's meticulously researched works, "Centennial Campaign: The Sioux War of 1876" (Old Army Press, 1976) and "Custer's Last Campaign: Mitch Boyer and the Little Bighorn Reconstructed" (University of Nebraska Press, 1991) are invaluable in reaching a contemporary understanding of the 1876 campaign and the battle. More recent accounts worthy of note are James Donovan's "A Terrible Glory: Custer and the Little Bighorn — The Last Great Battle of the American West" (Little, Brown and Company, 2008) and Nathaniel Philbrick's "The Last Stand: Custer, Sitting Bull, and the Battle of the Little Bighorn" (Viking, 2010). Both books are well researched, but at times take considerable poetic license in reconstructing events and dialog.

The archeological evidence turned up in the 1980s is analyzed and interpreted in Richard Allan Fox, Jr.'s "Archaeology, History, and Custer's Last Battle: The Little Big Horn Re-examined" (University of Oklahoma Press, 1993). Here, Fox argues that historical accounts need to be integrated with the archeological evidence, not the reverse, as is the usual custom. His conclusions that the heroic last stand is largely a myth and that Custer's men suffered a debilitating psychological collapse before being slaughtered by blood-thirsty warriors is, to say the least, controversial. Gregory Michno's "The Mystery of E Troop: Custer's Gray Horse Company at the Little Bighorn" (Mountain Press Publishing Company, 1994) used recent archeological digs to explode the myths surrounding the previously assumed fate of Troop E, thereby attacking Richard Fox's supposition that Custer's battalion fell in panic and confusion.

To put the Indian Wars in perspective, see Robert M. Utley's "Frontier Regulars: The United States Army and the Indian, 1866-1891" (Macmillan, 1973), which is a much more balanced account than Ralph K. Andrist's "The Long Death: The Last Days of the Plains Indians" (Macmillan, 1964).

Edward Tabor Linenthal's "Sacred Ground: Americans and Their Battlefields" (University of Illinois Press, 1991) devotes a chapter to the controversy over the interpretation of the battlefield at the Little Bighorn.

Finally, there are a number of other guides to the Civil War, Custer, Plains Forts, the Sioux War of 1876 and the Little Bighorn about which you should know:

Jeff Barnes is the author of two: "The Great Plains Guide to Custer: 85 Forts, Fights & Other Sites" (Stackpole Books, 2012) and "Forts of the Northern Plains: Guide to the Historic Military Posts of the Plains Indian Wars" (Stackpole Books, 2008).

Paul L. Hedren's "Traveler's Guide to the Great Sioux War" (Montana Historical Society Press, 1996) concentrates on the campaign of 1876 and is a fitting companion work to John Gray's "Centennial Campaign."

Robert M. Utley, "Little Bighorn Battlefield: A History and Guide to the Battle of the Little Bighorn: Custer Battlefield National Monument" (NPS Handbook, 1988) is available at the battlefield bookstore.

Two excellent Civil War battlefield guides are:

Frances H. Kennedy (ed.), "The Civil War Battlefield Guide" (The Conservation Fund, 1990; second edition, 1998) contains great maps.

Jeff Shaara, "Jeff Shaara's Civil War Battlefields: Discovering America's Hallowed Ground" (Ballantine, 2006) is by the acclaimed best-selling Civil War author.

ABOUT THE AUTHORS

Stephen T. Powers

Professor Stephen T. Powers is the author of *The March to Victory, A Guide to World War II Battles and Battlefields from London to the Rhine*. Along with Kevin Dennehy, he is the author of *The D-Day Assault, A Guide to the Normandy Landings after 70 Years*. A U.S. Naval Academy graduate, Powers was a history professor at the University of Northern Colorado for more than 30 years.

Kevin Dennehy

Kevin Dennehy has been a journalist for more than 29 years. He has written for daily newspapers and magazines. A retired Army National Guard colonel, Dennehy is a combat veteran of Afghanistan and Iraq.

NOTES

www.ingramcontent.com/pod-product-compliance
Lightning Source LLC
Chambersburg PA
CBHW061655040426
42446CB00010B/1752